# NATION OF NITWITS AND BARBARIANS

# BY THEODORE R. HALEY, MD

Note for Librarians: A cataloguing record for this book is available from Library and Archives Canada at www.collectionscanada.ca/amicus/index-e.html
ISBN 1-4251-0652-8

**PUBLISHING**™
*Offices in Canada, USA, Ireland and UK*

**Book sales for North America and international:**
Trafford Publishing, 6E–2333 Government St.,
Victoria, BC V8T 4P4 CANADA
phone 250 383 6864 (toll-free 1 888 232 4444)
fax 250 383 6804; email to orders@trafford.com
**Book sales in Europe:**
Trafford Publishing (UK) Limited, 9 Park End Street, 2nd Floor
Oxford, UK OX1 1HH UNITED KINGDOM
phone +44 (0)1865 722 113 (local rate 0845 230 9601)
facsimile +44 (0)1865 722 868; info.uk@trafford.com
**Order online at:**
trafford.com/06-2410

10 9 8 7 6 5 4 3 2

# NATION OF NITWITS AND BARBARIANS

# BY THEODORE R. HALEY, MD

# ABOUT THE AUTHOR

Theodore R. Haley MD was born and raised in Tacoma WA, graduated from Amherst College in 1944 and the U of Rochester School of Medicine in 1947. He served in the Navy in WWII and the Army in the Korean War, totaling 20 years, retiring as a Lt. Colonel. He practiced general surgery in Tacoma and surgical critical care in Chicago

And became an Associate Professor of Surgery at the U of Il College of Medicine in Rockford Il in 2003.

# CONTENTS:

6

# INTRODUCTION
# TRH in Amsterdam

"What's my chance of becoming a Dutch citizen? You're the most civilized country in the world," I said to the lady official.

"Yes, we know," she replied.

" Compared to you we Americans are barbarians," I said.

"Yes, we know that, too," she replied.

" Here, you have marijuana in the bars and taverns and over there elegant brothels," I quipped, pointing down the main avenue.

" Yes, and if someone wants to kill himself taking drugs, why not let him do it? " she replied.

Then, she added that Holland is a small country and already has too many inhabitants and my reasons weren't good enough.

The place: Amsterdam

The year: 2000

What a subject for a book! I thought later. Comparing US and Dutch attitudes and practices.

# Part I
# THE MOST CIVILIZED NATION
## Live and let Live

The Dutch are a truly remarkable people. More forward thinking than any other nation. Scandinavians probably come second, but are way behind the Dutch.

Adjectives such as tolerant, progressive, liberal, compassionate, understanding, civilized and pragmatic are used to describe them. "Live and let live" aptly and succinctly summarizes their philosophy, " If you leave me alone, I'll leave you alone.

This way we'll have fewer conflicts," to use their terms, also applies well.

How did the Dutch get that way?

It started in the 17th century, when the Netherlands gave asylum to people who were persecuted in their own countries, mainly for their religious beliefs. Also, since sailing the seven seas in pursuit of commerce became the basis for their considerable prosperity, it was necessary to learn other languages and accept differences. As the Dutch became more sophisticated, they gave up much of their early Catholic and Calvinist beliefs. Now that most people are not church-goers, Christians and members of other faiths make up about only a third of the population, freeing the majority from religious restrictions.

Progressive legislation goes back many years in the Netherlands. The death penalty, now illegal in the EU, was abolished in 1870 in the Netherlands, the first European nation to do so. The sale of limited amounts of soft drugs, like marijuana, has been legal for many years in the Netherlands. Prostitution was legalized in 2000, and same-sex marriage and euthanasia in 2001. The Dutch attitude about many of these things is that it will happen anyway, whether or not they prohibit them. So why not legalize them?

## PROSTITUTION

Prostitution has long been tolerated in the Netherlands under the gedoogbeleid (policy of toleration) with the reasoning that the world's "oldest profession" has proven impossible to ban by any government. Indeed, in where it is banned it is usually the prostitute who is the victim, and as the easiest target, the one who suffers criminal prosecution instead of the client or the pimp. In an effort to stop the exploitation of sex workers, prostitution in brothels was legalized in the Netherlands in October 2000. This also gave the government the opportunity to tax prostitution and for prostitutes to pay social security and receive benefits and pensions. By legitimizing prostitutes as workers, it is viewed that this will help remove control from the criminal element and make it easier to clamp down on exploitation.

Window prostitution is the most visible form, though it only takes up about 20% of the entire sex industry in the Netherlands. Windows are rented for 8-hour shifts for some 60-150 euros (depending on time and place), which includes closed circuit security. Fifteen to twenty minutes of sex cost about 40 to 50 euros (though prices can go both higher and lower according to the service; usually, 15-20 minutes is what is called a " suck and a fuck") Despite the legalization, some of the working women are still illegal immigrants. However, they cannot work in the windows, since they are required to have European Union passports in order to rent one.

Some municipalities in the Netherlands would like a "zero-tolerance" policy for brothel on moral grounds, but by law this is not possible. However, regulations, including restrictions in number and location, are common. Whether a zero-tolerance policy on urban planning grounds is slowed is still unclear.

There are twelve red-light districts with window prostitution in the Netherlands. A thirteenth (Spijkerkwartler in Arnhem) was closed down in 2005. The largest and best known is DeWallen in Amsterdam, also known as Walletjes or Rosse Buurt.

Prostitutes must be at least 18, while for non-commercial sex the age of consent is 16. Clients must be at least 16. Prostitutes are considered bona fide entrepreneurs; they pay taxes and are otherwise treated like any other self-employed tradesperson. Advertising the services is likewise tolerated. Health and social services are readily available, but the women are not required to undergo regular health checks. The women are usually self-employed, but not always/

An article in Le Monde 1997 found that 80% of prostitutes in the Netherlands were foreigners and 70% had no immigration papers, suggesting that at least some were victims of sex trafficking, particularly forced prostitution. The Netherlands is one of a number of countries in Europe for trafficked women (many of whom are led by organized criminals that they are being offered work in hotels or restaurants or in child care and are forced into prostitution with the threat or actual use of violence).

In an effort to crack down on forced prostitution, a campaign was launched in 2005 in magazines through posters put up around the red-light districts encouraging clients to report signs of coercion. The poster has an eye-catching silhouette of a spike-heeled prostititute with long hair leaning back, but on closer inspection, another picture reveals a gun being held to the female's head. The caption reads, "Have you seen the signals? Fear, bruises, no "pleasure in the job", it then goes on to offer a phone number which clients can call anonymously.

## SEX EDUCATION

Sex at a young age, is another good example of the same tolerance. Undesirable according to many, but treated pragmatically by the Dutch.

Kids will have sex, whether you like it or not. So, at 12 years old, they get education and can go to a clinic to get contraceptives. Anonymously, if they want. Their parents won't know.

Does this stimulate the Dutch adolescents to have sex at a younger age, as critics might claim? No. Dutch youngsters have their first sexual experience rather late. And more importantly, the number of abortions and unwanted pregnancies is the lowest in the world.

## ABORTION

The Netherlands took an ever-increasing liberal view concerning abortion, especially when abortion became possible in other countries. Politicians were about equally divided in conservatives, and progressives in favor of abortion. A safe and reliable Abortion Service, initiated by a small group of medical pioneers, was well established when at last in 1981 the Abortion Act was passed. It allows abortions to be done in hospitals and dedicated abortion clinics in the Netherlands. A hospital or abortion clinic may be licensed for first-trimester abortions only, or for both first and second-trimester abortions (up till 23 weeks). In the clinics abortions were mostly done under local anesthesia. Nowadays conscious sedation is available for those women who want it. The hospitals, being of a somewhat conservative nature, generally prefer general anesthesia. At this moment there are some twenty abortion clinics in the Netherlands. By law, abortion up till 23 weeks is available on demand to every woman in the Netherlands. The doctor should confirm the women's emergency situation, check if the woman considered other options, and comes voluntary. For Netherlands subjects and foreign residents the service is free, the clinics are paid on a real cost basis by the Government, which ensures their non-profit character. The only condition is that the patient discusses her case with a doctor and that she waits five days after this discussion to discuss meticulously her decision. A clinic may accept a patient on her oral declaration that she has met these requirements, and proof is not necessary. The woman decides herself whether she wants her pregnancy to be terminated regardless of the advice of her doctor. A minor (under 16 years) needs approval of one of her parents or her guardian. If a minor is estranged from her parents, a Court Justice may approve in loco parentis. If the parents refuse approval, the Court may overrule their refusal if that is considered in the interest of the minor. This is the same procedure as in the case of parents refusing a child to undergo a necessary operation or blood transfusion. An appeal on religious reasons is generally not accepted.

A doctor may refuse to cooperate with an abortion but he is not allowed to refuse the woman the possibility. For instance, denying that she is pregnant till her pregnancy is too far advanced is considered a medical misdemeanor. If he is against abortion, he must tell the woman and advise her to see another doctor.

Although gratis abortion virtually on demand is available to every woman, the number of abortions in the Netherlands is one of the lowest in the world. The friendly and understanding way the woman is encountered prevents psychological problems and motivates her to accept contraceptive advice. If a woman comes the third time for an abortion, she is treated in exactly the same way without reproof. She is advised that she is welcome to come again but that she can better take contraceptives or have a sterilization done. This attitude works. Regret is seldom. In the southern Catholic part of the country, the abortion rate is relatively higher than in the liberal northern part. Also contraception is worse, and feelings of guilt after the intervention are more frequent.

Since 1970 more than a million abortions have been done in the Netherlands, most in the abortion clinics, less in hospitals. This number is so great because the Netherlands rather than the UK became the abortion country in Europe so that more foreign than Dutch women were treated. The number of foreign patients has declined considerably while abortion gradually became available in other countries. The number of complications has remained low. Only one fatal complication occurred in one of the clinics, and three fatalities were reported from hospitals, all due to complications of anesthesia. If all patients who underwent an abortion would have delivered a child, the number of fatalities would have been 88, the maternal death rate in the Netherlands. It is therefore safer to have an abortion than a delivery. This interesting aspect of termination of pregnancy is never taken into account by pro-life activists, who keep hammering on the dangers of abortion.

Teens in the US are nearly 7 times more likely to have abortions than teens in the Netherlands. The teen pregnancy rate is 9 times higher and the gonorrhea rate is an astounding 74 times higher in the US than in the Netherlands. Three reasons: The Dutch have a more open approach toward sexuality, a later sexual debut, and fewer sexual partners.

## DRUG POLICY

The drug policy of the Netherlands is based on two principles:

1. Drug use is a public health issue, not a criminal matter.

2. A distinction between hard drugs and soft drugs exists.

It is a pragmatic policy. Most policymakers in the Netherlands believe that if a problem has proved to be unstoppable, it is better to try controlling it instead of continuing to enforce laws that have shown to be unable to stop the problem.

Most other countries take the point of view that drugs are bad and must be outlawed, whether that course of action yields any results or not. This has caused friction between the Netherlands and other countries, most notably with France and Germany. As of 2004, Belgium seems to be moving toward the Dutch model,and a few local German legislators are calling for experiments based on the Dutch model. Switzerland has had long and heated parliamentary debates about whether to follow the Dutch model, but finally decided against it in 2004; currently aballot initiative is in the works on the question.

A distinction is drawn between hard drugs (which bear "unacceptable" risks; e.g.cocaine, heroin, and ecstasy) and hard drugs such as the psychodelic psilocybin mushrooms as well as cannabis products: hashish and marijuana (as defined in the Dutch Opium Act). The distinction is drawn on whether the substance is onlypsychologically addictive (i.e. producing no worse effect than moderate cravingwhen withdrawn) or also physically addictive (i.e. there is solid proof the drugcould cause dangerous withdrawal symptoms and/or lasting physical damage).One of the main aims of this policy is to separate the markets for soft and hard drugs sothat soft drug users are less likely to come into contact with hard drugs. This policyalso aims to take the soft drug market out of the hands of criminals, thus reducing crime.

The use of soft drugs in general is not prohibited, on the general principle of self-determination in matters of the body. Specifically, it is not illegal to hurt yourself. However, you remain liable for the consequences of your actions. Because of this, users are not prosecuted for prosecution of small quantities of soft drugs ("for personal use") Driving under the influence of drugs is nevertheless prohibited, as is being under the influence in public (of either alcohol or drugs), mainly from a public nuisance perspective.

So-called "coffee shops" are allowed to sell soft drugs openly, and to keep supplies greater than the amounts allowed by law for personal use. The coffee shops' wholesale suppliers, however, are still criminalized. In practice, the limit of the "for personal use" clause is 5 cannabis plants per person for growing, or possession of 5 grams of hashish of marijuana per person. Example of sentence in 2004 for possession of 360 grams: confiscation and a fine of 750 euros. Coffee shops pay taxes just like any other business, though there are some special exemptions for them, mostly because they cannot show receipts for their supply of marijuana.

Large-scale dealing, production, import and export are prosecuted to the fullest extent of the law, even if this does not supply end users or coffee shops with more than the allowed amounts. Exactly how coffee shops get their supplies is rarely investigated, however. What is certain is that coffee shops do sell cannabis that comes from countries where cannabis is illegal. Large suppliers tend to be criminals motivated by profit who do not make the distinction between hard and soft drugs. Hence, the soft drug policy, by failing to address the issue of supply, has made the Netherlands the main centre for hard drug trafficking in Europe. Creating a highly controlled, legal production chain for cannabis to combat this problem has been proposed by a number of Dutch politicians over the last few years. By the end of 2005, the majority of the Dutch Parliament was in favor of an experiment with controlled cultivation and production of cannabis. It is still uncertain when and how this experiment will take place, due to judicial issues.

Despite the high priority given by the Dutch government to fighting narcotics trafficking, the Netherlands continue to be an important transit point for drugs entering Europe, a major producer of amphetamines and other synthetic drugs, and an important consumer of illicit drugs. The export of the synthetic drug Ecstasy to the US during 1999 reached unprecedented proportions. The Netherlands' special synthetic drug unit, set up in 1997 to coordinate the fight against designer drugs, appears to be successful. The government has stepped up border controls and intensified cooperation with neighboring countries.

Although drug use, as opposed to trafficking, is seen primarily as a public health issue, responsibility for drug policy is shared by both the Ministry of Health, Welfare, and Sports, and the Ministry of Justice.

In contrast with most countries' policies, the Dutch policy

has yielded positive results in the war against drugs. The Netherlands spends more than 130 million euros annually on facilities for addicts, of which about 50% goes to drug addicts. The Netherlands has extensive demand reduction programs, reaching about 90% of the country's 25,000 to 28,000 hard drug users. The number of hard drug users has stabilized in the past few years, and their average age has risen to 38 years. The number of drug-related deaths in the country remains the lowest in Europe.

Despite the legalization of soft drugs, use of cannabis in the Netherlands is not higher than most other countries in Western Europe: 9.7% of young males consume cannabis at least once a month, which rates the Netherlands 7th in the EU after Cyprus (23.3%), Spain (16.4%), United Kingdom (15.8%), France (13.2%), Italy (10.9%) and Germany (9.9%). Some critics say that the legalization of soft drugs often leads to quicker consumption of hard drugs. Yes, the percentage of the population which consumes cocaine in the Netherlands is still lower than that of the United Kingdom, Spain, and Italy. The situation is similar for hard drugs.

## EUTHANASIA

The Netherlands legalized euthanasia in 2001, the first country in the world to do so. The procedure must be carried out in medically appropriate fashion. Persons 16 years old and older can make a written request for termination of life which the physician may carry out. The request need not be made in conjunction with any particular medical condition. A parent or guardian must be involved in the decision but need not approve for persons between 16 and 18. Children younger than that must have a parent's or guardian's approval.

A person may qualify for assisted suicide if the doctor

believes the patient's suffering is lasting and unbearable and he or she must have the agreement of a colleague. There is no requirement that the suffering be physical or the patient be terminally ill. All oversight of the procedure is conducted after the death of the patient by a regional review committee consisting of a physician, a legal specialist, and an expert on ethics. The procedure is an injection rendering the patient unconscious followed by a medication that stops the heart. The law does not require the patient to be a Dutch resident.

It is also legal for doctors to end the lives of newborn babies if the parents agree and the infants have no chance of survival, or must be on life support indefinitely. Examples include extremely premature births, severe brain damage, severe cases of spina bifida, etc.

## SAME-SEX MARRIAGE

In 2001 the Netherlands enacted the world's most comprehensive legal recognition of gay rights allowing same sex couples to marry and giving them the same rights as heterosexuals regarding adoption. The only restriction is that same sex couples can only adopt Dutch children. And foreign same sex couples cannot come to the Netherlands to marry unless one of them lives there.

## POLYGAMY

The first legal marriage of three consenting adults in the Netherlands occurred in 2005 when a 46 –year-old-man married his wife's girlfriend, claiming he loved them both. Polygamy will undoubtedly regain the legal status it once had in most western countries in the far distant future. And it will also occur among three homosexuals, Someday.

## DUTCH TOLERANCE PUT TO THE TEST

There was concern that Dutch society's longstanding tradition of tolerance was under threat when the homosexual anti-immigration politician Pim Fortuyn was assassinated in 2002. Anxiety over increased racial tension has intensified further since the murder in 2004 of Theo Van Gogh who had made a controversial film on the position of women in Islamic society. A violent extremist later confessed and was jailed for life. Since Mr. Van Gogh's killing, the government has hardened its line on immigration and failed asylum seekers.

It has put into effect an **entrance** test that would-be immigrants are forced to take, the first of its kind in the world, which consists of a 105-minute movie available at all of the 138 Dutch embassies. A CD-ROM and picture album of famous Dutch people is also included. The camera focuses on two gay men kissing in a park. Later, a topless woman walks onto a crowded beach. Before being approved for immigration, the applicant is questioned about his or her reaction to the test and there must be acceptance and approval of such Dutch social practices. This test and other policies have reduced immigration by a third.

## HEALTH CARE

"The Dutch health care system, unlike that of other countries, provides care for all citizens at a highly advanced level, without exceptions."

" Almost all patients (99.4%) have health care insurance, and 100% of the population is insured for the cost of protracted illnesses. There are no financial incentives for hospitals, physicians, or family members to stop the care of patients. Moreover, the right of patients to health care on the basis of their insurance will override budget and other financial agreements."

## Palliative care

Pain and palliation centres are attached to all hospitals. Other countries, by comparison, have costly but relatively few such centres (normally known as "hospices")

During the Nazi occupation, Dutch doctors went to concentration camps rather than divulge the names of their patients. This is one of the factors that increase the relationship of trust between doctors and patients, to a much higher level than in most other countries. Moreover, most patients know their doctor well, and over a considerable time period. And most die at home under the care of their general practitioners.

The Dutch rate is very high on social services, including the war on poverty, and is among the highest in EU and UN ranking. And the AARP magazine rates the Netherlands #1 on care and services to the elderly.

## MARRIAGE AND FAMILY

Many couples live together before or instead of getting married. Since January 1998, same-sex partnerships have been legally recognized. Same-sex partners are given rights that heterosexual couples enjoy, such as taxation benefits and inheritance rights. The Dutch have strong families, which are moderate in size. Most have one or two children, but southern (Catholic) families tend to be a bit larger. Single parents are common. Grandparents live on their own or in a nursing home. People generally live close to extended family. Many holidays emphasize family gatherings. As is the case throughout Europe, both parents often work outside the home. Dutch women often keep their own surnames after marriage, and they are entering the job market at a heightened pace. About 40.2% (1998) of the labor force is female, and one-fifth of all legislative seats are held by women.

## EDUCATION

Schooling is free and compulsory between the ages of five and sixteen. Children may be enrolled for an optional year at age four. Primary education ends at age twelve. Students may go to a Catholic, Protestant, Muslim, or "non-religious" school, but the basic curriculum is the same. Secondary school begins with two years of "basic education." All students study the basic 15 subjects that emphasize practical applications of knowledge. After that, they can choose between different types of high school, ranging from pre-vocational to pre-university. The number of years varies with the program. Higher education is subsidized by the government. There are 13 universities, the oldest of which, Leiden, was founded by William of Orange in 1575.

## FOREIGN RELATIONS

The Dutch are very internationally minded. They are very supportive of the UN and various UN agencies. And along with the Benelux (Belgium, Netherlands, and Luxembourg) nations, they were members of the European

Economic Community unions and the European Coal and Steel Community, which later evolved into the EU. The euro soon replaced the guilder as the Dutch national currency. The Netherlands is a parliamentary democracy under a constitutional monarch, Queen Beatrix, whose birthday is the grandest celebration of the year. Amsterdam is the official capital but the Hague is the seat of government and home of the international Court of Justice.

The bitter experience of invasion and occupation in World War 11 and the killing of many thousands of Jews, gypsies, homosexuals, mentally retarded and disabled individuals by the Nazis persuaded the Dutch to abandon neutrality and become a leading supporter of international cooperation. Dutch armed forces have participated in a number of tasks outside the Netherlands including sending troops to Iraq, Afghanistan, and other NATO and humanitarian assignments.

In addition to the Netherlands being famous as a land of windmills, tulips, wooden shoes, and bicycles, and because one-third of the land is below sea level, the Dutch have had to build dykes since Roman times, and have gotten very good at it. So good that the US used Dutch water experts and their pumps to help manage Hurricane Katrina flooding. Global warming and rising sea levels are viewed by the Dutch as imminent threats to their national security, and they are devising solutions and innovations to cope.

# PART 2:
# THE US AND SOCIAL AND ECONOMIC ISSUES
## War and Torture

When George Bush was asked if he had asked his father about going to war, he replied that he hadn't but he had asked his heavenly father who told him to go to war. One wonders whether George Bush really believes in god or is it a ruse to capture the hearts and minds (and votes) of the millions of god fearing Christians in the red states. Judging from his ignorance about how to pronounce the word nuclear, it's quite believable that he really believes in god. His determination to go to war certainly overcame all the many reasons not to go to war, such as his secretary of state, Colin Powell, being opposed to it. And Hans Blix and others not finding any weapons of mass destruction in Iraq. And Joseph Wilson going to Niger and reporting no materials there for making a nuclear weapon, as had been suspected for sale to Saddam Hussein. And if Bush personally didn't recall the disaster of fighting a guerilla war in Vietnam, why did his advisors not remind him? Also, tell him about the certainty of suicide bombing by Muslim extremists as their way of promptly going to heaven? And the probability that the Kurds, Sunnis and

Shiites would never bury the hatchet and form a workable democracy? And that 3 thousand or more American troops would die and many thousands wounded? And that 100,000 innocent men, women and children would die as a result of the war? It's projected that close to one trillion dollars will be spent. Dollars that are sorely needed for health care, education, social security, etc., etc., etc. But, more surprising than George Bush not realizing what he was getting us into, was the Senate authorizing him to go to war. Including several Democrats! What were they thinking about? Were they in some kind of trance?

And a shocking side development—the torture of prisoners at Abu Ghraib!! Also Guantanamo and Afghanistan!! Have we forgotten about the Geneva Convention international agreement against torture? No wonder most of the world no longer respects us.

There can no longer be any doubt: The American war in Iraq---an unprovoked, unnecessary, unlawful invasion that has turned into a colonial-style occupation—is a moral and political catastrophe. The long-term damage to our foreign policy and standing in the world is incalculable. It has bred a new generation of religious extremists, dangerously heightened sectarian tensions in the Islamic world, strengthened Iran's hand

In Iraq and in matters of nuclear diplomacy, and created a serious threat to the world's oil supply---all the while undermining American authority in the region and straining the US military to the breaking point. And as recent events have made clear, Iraq is on the verge of a full-scale war.

The best solution is for the US to get out of Iraq now, and persuade the UN to assist the Iraqis in rebuilding their physical, cultural, and institutional infrastructure to the level of a modern nation. Oil revenues should be used for the sole benefit of the Iraqi people, particularly the poor, not to enrich multi-national corporations. All assistance should be provided within the context of specific requests and with the final determination made by Iraqis.

Militarily speaking, America is now a giant, spending almost as much as the rest of the world combined. The pentagon's budget is larger than the entire economy of Russia. It is also the largest source of waste, fraud, and mismanagement in the federal government. And we now have troops in 130 0f the world's 200 countries, including Iraq, Afghanistan, the Philippines, Sudan, Somalia, the Republic of Georgia, and many others.

## GLOBAL WARMING

Most scientists believe that most of the global warming seen over the past 50 years was caused by humans burning fossil fuels, land clearing, and agriculture, thus adding carbon dioxide and other greenhouse gases to the atmosphere. They are predicting an increase of 1.4 to 5.8 degrees centigrade between 1990 and 2100, causing a rise in sea level, changes in the amount and pattern of precipitation, floods, droughts, heat waves, hurricanes, lower agricultural yields, glacier retreats, reduced summer stream flows, and biological extinctions. The most catastrophic effects of global warming include increasingly strong and frequent hurricanes, causing great loss of life and financial assets running into billions of dollars per year. The rising sea levels, currently 1 to 2 mm per year, soon will have serious impacts on low-lying countries such as Bangladesh, Vietnam, China, India, Thailand, the Philippines, Indonesia, Egypt, the Netherlands, and the small Pacific island nations.

Infectious disease patterns will probably change, causing disease and death from malaria, Hantavirus, hemorrhagic fever, tularemia, and rabies, which will require extensive preventive and treatment changes. Flora and fauna such as penguins, polar bears, and snowy owls will be hit hard while others will flourish.

Beneficial effects of global warming are few but do exist. For instance, rising $CO_2$ increasing the metabolism in most plants and warmer temperatures in colder climates would increase agricultural output. Also less energy would be needed to heat living spaces. Finally, the Northwest Passage would be open in the summertime for shipping between Europe and Asia, especially helpful for tankers too big to go through the Panama Canal.

What is being done about it?

In 1997 the UN sponsored a convention in Kyoto, Japan, that created a document called the Kyoto Treaty, requiring 35 industrialized nations to curb emissions of carbon dioxide and 5 other gases that act like a greenhouse, trapping heat in the atmosphere, by 5% below 1990 levels until 2012. Nations were given til 2005 to fix it and 160 that had ratified the treaty, including 55 industrialized nations, even Russia, did so. But not the US, having withdrawn from consideration of the treaty in 20001, and not offering any other approach for international consideration.

As a result of national governmental inaction, the governors of states, mayors of cities, and private companies have admirably taken up the cause and instituted many measures to reduce emissions, such as making more efficient autos and hybrids, making ethanol from corn and cellulose to add to gasoline, cleaning dirty coal fired plants, erecting wind turbines and rooftop solar generators. building nuclear power plants, encouraging public transit, ride sharing, walking and biking, etc.

George Bush argued that since Kyoto exempted 80% of the world, including China and India, the cost would be too large, causing "serious harm to the US economy". The

US, in spite of the fact that it has only 5% of the world's population and 'only 3% of the world's oil reserves, consumes 25% of the world's oil supply, but continues to thumb its nose at international cooperation and remains embarrassingly isolated in the worldwide effort to reduce global warming.

## HEALTH CARE

Forty-seven million people in the US without health insurance? Incredible! Disgraceful! Shameful! All the other industrialized nations provide health insurance to all their citizens, but not the US! What happened? How did we get this way?

Harry Truman tried to create a national health insurance system. Public opinion was initially on his side. Jill Quadagno's book One Nation, Uninsured tells us that in 1945, 75 percent of Americans favored national health insurance. If Truman had succeeded, universal coverage for everyone, not just the elderly, would today be an accepted part of the social contract.

But Truman failed. Special interests, especially the American Medical Association and Southern politicians who feared that national insurance would lead to racially integrated hospitals, triumphed. Sixty years later, the patchwork system that evolved in the absence of national health insurance is unraveling. The cost of health care is exploding, the number of uninsured is growing, and corporations that still provide employee coverage are groaning under the strain. So the time will soon be ripe for another try at universal coverage. Public opinion is already favorable: a 2003 Pew poll found that 72 percent of Americans favored government-guaranteed health insurance for all. But special interests will, once again stand in the way. And the big debate among would-be reformers is how to deal with those interests, especially the insurance companies. These companies played a secondary role in Truman's failure but since have become a seemingly invincible lobby.

Let's ignore those who believe that private medical accounts—basically tax shelters for the healthy and wealthy- can solve our health care problems through the magic of the marketplace. The intellectually serious debate is between those who believe that the government should simply provide basic health insurance for everyone and those proposing a more complex, indirect approach that preserves a central role for private health insurance companies.

A system in which the government provides universal health insurance is often referred to as " single payer", but I like Ted Kennedy's slogan " Medicare for All." It reminds voters that America already has a highly successful, popular single-payer program, albeit only for the elderly. It shows that we're talking about government insurance, not government-provided health care. And it makes it clear that like Medicare (but unlike Canada's system), a U.S. national health insurance system would allow individuals with the means and inclination to buy their own medical care.

The great advantage of universal government-provided health insurance is lower costs. Canada's government-run insurance system has much less bureaucracy and much lower administrative costs than our largely private system. Medicare has much lower administrative costs than private insurance. The reason is that single-payer systems don't devote large resources to screening out high-risk clients or charging them higher fees. The savings from a single-payer system would probably exceed $200 billion a year, far more than the cost of covering all those now uninsured.

Nonetheless, most reform proposals out there-even proposals from liberal groups like the Century Foundation and the Center for American Progress-reject a simple single-payer approach. Instead, they call for some combination of mandates and subsidies to help everyone buy insurance from private insurers. Some people, not all of them right-wingers, fear that a single-payer system would hurt innovation. But the main reason is these proposals give private insurance a big role is the belief that the insurers must be appeased. That belief is rooted in recent history. Bill Clinton's health care plan failed in large part because of a dishonest but devastating lobbying and advertising campaign financed by the health insurance industry-remember Harry and Louise? And the lesson many people took from that defeat is that any future health care proposal must buy off the insurance lobby.

But I think that's the wrong lesson. The Clinton plan actually preserved a big role for private insurers; the industry attacked it all the same. And the plan's complexity, which was largely a result of attempts to placate interest groups, made it hard to sell to the public. So I would argue that good economics is also good politics: reformers will do best with a straightforward single-payer plan, which offers maximum savings, and unlike the Clinton plan, can easily be explained. We need to do this one right. If reform fails again, we'll be on the way to a radically unequal society, in which all but the most affluent Americans face the constant risk of financial ruin and even premature death because they can't pay their medical bills.

## HIV/AIDS

George Bush's Global Gag Rule seriously undermined prevention and treatment of the worldwide HIV/AIDS pandemic crisis because US health agencies refused to sign it, denying them access to USAID donated condoms, one of the crucial weapons in the HIV/AIDS prevention battle, thus increasing the chance that people, especially teens, will engage in risky sex, greatly increasing their odds of getting HIV.

Tragically, 38 million people are now infected with HIV- with those aged 15 to 24 accounting for almost half of all new cases. Mother to child transmission of HIV is especially serious. Approximately 1700 young children become HIV positive every day of the year. UNICEF has developed an effective program for preventing mother to child transmission, HIV testing, and retroviral drugs for those infected during the late months of pregnancy or during birth, and afterwards the best methods to care for and feed the child. But the number of children orphaned by HIV/AIDS is astronomically high.

One bright spot in the US's dismal approach to this disease are the dollars pledged by the Gates and Buffett Foundations, 2 of America's wealthiest persons, providing life-saving treatment to hundreds of thousands of AIDS patients, mainly in Africa.

## SHAME ON ORGAN TRANSPLANT SURGEONS!!!

Compassion they lack!!

A couple of years ago, there were over 85,000 patients waiting for organ transplants in this country, but less than 15,000 transplants were performed, mainly because the organs were not available. Not enough relatives or other persons volunteered to donate, including those freshly dead from accidents and other causes, even though many drivers volunteered their organs by signing the agreement on the back of their drivers licenses.

Unlike many other countries, it's illegal in the US to

sell your organs. As a result, 61,700 Americans die every year waiting for a transplant. As embarrassing as it is that the US executes more criminals than China, Iran, and Vietnam, and that we have executed over 1,000 persons since 1976, when the Supreme Court validated the states' execution rights, we could achieve at least a modicum of respect and forgiveness in the eyes of the world if we put this uncivilized practice to at least some good use, such as transplanting the organs of the executed to some merciful and compassionate use, such as organ transplantation.

At least a dozen afflicted patients could have their lives extended by harvesting the organs of a single healthy criminal whose kidneys, liver, heart, lungs, intestines, bone marrow, etc. were transplanted. At least a tiny amount of atonement or amends could have been made for the guilty person's horrible action of taking a life. And this donation should help the aggrieved relatives forgive.

If this process became standard practice in the US, at least 700 lives per year would be saved!

Then why, oh why, haven't doctors, especially transplant surgeons and their professional organizations appealed to any of the three dozen states that still execute, to allow organ harvesting of those executed? When questioned about this matter, the doctors have countered by saying that they're afraid of being accused of killing innocent persons for their organs, like happens in Asia. The best response to this irrational answer is to accuse them of being worried about what some nut will say about them, than employing the utmost compassion for their patients, and harvesting these organs for transplant. And compassion should be every doctor's number one concern!

# THE DRUG WAR

## Marijuana

On April 19, 2005, the Canadian government gave conditional approval to prescription sale of a medicine made from extracts of marijuana plants ingested as an oral spray.

While the US blocked privately-funded research, a British pharmaceutical company developed a cannabis extract spray that supplements existing non-smoking delivery systems such as vaporization.

The risks versus the benefits of alternative methods need to be established. But the US government is obstructing the science because it fears the results will demonstrate an acceptable risk/ benefit ratio even for smoked marijuana.

This research would be welcomed by the 14,600,000 Americans who currently use marijuana socially or medically.

Like many herbal remedies, marijuana is an excellent medicine. It improves the appetite of anorexics and those suffering from AIDS or various cancers, lowers eyeball pressure in glaucoma, and causes euphoria and diminished anxiety. It can be used episodically without evidence of psychological or social dysfunction. No withdrawal syndrome occurs when the drug is discontinued.

Pot is no more addicting than caffeine and much less so than nicotine and alcohol. Of the 65 to 70 million Americans who have tried cannabis, about 2 to 3% are daily or near-daily users, and very few of them are addicts. But, like cigarettes, prolonged daily pot smoking is hard on the lungs and in time may cause emphysema or lung cancer.

If marijuana is so therapeutic and benign, why can't US doctors everywhere prescribe marijuana for anorexic patients, or those undergoing cancer chemotherapy,

HIV/AIDS treatment, or other disorders? It's because the Republican-led Congress has shown no sign of passing a medical marijuana law. So, it's been up to individual states to do so, and many have.

It is encouraging to know that most states are getting smart and legalizing medical marijuana and decriminalizing possession of small amounts of pot, thus allowing cops to focus on serious criminals instead of recreational users, build fewer prisons, end the scarring of young lives by arrest and imprisonment for behavior that does no harm, and helps doctors treat anorexic patients legally.

One study found that since it began treating pot possession like jaywalking in 1976, California has saved at least $1 billion. And why not regulate marijuana like alcohol?

Marijuana is far safer than alcohol because it does not stimulate aggressiveness and is not nearly as addictive.

### Reasons to Legalize it

- To save $7.7 billion in enforcement costs.

- To produce $6.2 billion in tax revenue(which could be used to pay for education, treatment and prevention for all drugs).

- To deprive cartels and gangs of a major source of revenue.

- To separate marijuana from far more dangerous illegal drugs, ending the "gateway" to drug dealers we now have.

- To reduce hypocrisy and make drug education more credible and effective.

- To end prisons doing far more damage to users than the drug itself.

• To end the breaking of the law by otherwise law-abiding citizens, especially the more than 900.000 children under 18 years old who buy and resell marijuana.

• To remove major barriers to research for medical use.

• To reduce violence in general and safeguard law enforcers.

The most sensible and rational solution would be to tax it and sell it like alcohol in liquor outlets to customers old enough to by alcoholic beverages.

## Hard Drugs

Launched by President Nixon in 1971, the drug war is now in its fourth decade and is costing the country $69 billion and 1.5 million people are arrested every year!! This accounts for almost half a million of the 2 million people behind bars, the largest in the world! More than all the people jailed for crimes in the UK, France, Germany, Italy, and Spain put together! And they have a larger total population!! And of the 1.5 million drug-related arrests, a full 1.2 million are for possession only. Touching only a small fraction of the nation's estimated 28 million drug users, these arrests fall disproportionately on the poor.

Many arrests for possession occur because of some other violation such as prostitution, theft, speeding, loitering, disorderly conduct, etc. Three-fourths of them are black or Latino, though their drug use is no higher than among whites.

Despite all the time, energy and resources devoted to prosecuting the war on drugs, 3 out of 4 Americans agree that it's a complete failure. And drugs are more potent, cheaper and easier to obtain than ever.

In the world-over, about 5% or 200 million people use Hard or soft drugs, and about 30% or 160 million of those smoke pot. About 30% of adults smoke tobacco and about half drink alcohol. So, the problem is definitely worldwide.

The solution is not easy to come by. Several EU nations including the Netherlands, Italy, Spain, and Portugal have stopped arresting for possession of small amounts of hard drugs, cocaine being the most common. Heroin, Amphetamines, and Ecstasy are also used. The rates of addiction are about the same as in the US, but treatment is more available.

If drugs like heroin, cocaine, meth, etc. were decriminalized, would it lead to an explosion of hard drug use? The answer is "No!" Italy, Spain and Portugal have decriminalized personal use of all drugs and have found very little increase in their use. Mexico considered doing so, but was persuaded against it by the Bush Administration.

An unfortunate, shameful, and embarrassing fact related to the US prohibition of marijuana is that it's illegal for farmers to grow hemp in this country. Because it's improperly classified as a "drug", industrial hemp is non-psychoactive, low THC variety of the cannabis activa plant, and is widely used to make utensils, baskets, and many other articles in other countries. Presidents Washington and Jefferson both grew it and the Declaration of Independence was printed on paper made from it. Several agricultural states are now seeking its legalization.

## Law Enforcement Against Prohibition

The membership of LEAP believe that to save lives, and lower the rates of disease, crime, and addiction, as well as to conserve tax dollars, we must end drug prohibition.

LEAP members feel the role of law enforcement

should be to protect and serve. That means we should be interested in lowering the incidence of death, crime, and drug addiction- four categories made infinitely worse by the war on drugs. To do that we must end prohibition and legalize drugs---Legalize All drugs so that we can control and regulate them and keep them out of the hands of our children.

When officers arrest rapists or robbers they make our communities safer for everyone, but when they arrest drug dealers they simply create job openings for hundreds of people willing to take those jobs in order the obscene profits made available as a result of drug prohibition.

After nearly 4 decades of fighting the war on drugs, at a cost of more than a trillion dollars; after arresting 9 million non-violent drug-law-offenders in the last six years; after quadrupling our prison population to 2.2 million inmates--- Today drugs are cheaper, easier to get, and far more potent than they were when we started this war in 1970. That is a failed public policy.

110 million people in the US above the age of 12 have used an illegal drug. If we arrested them all, there would only be two kinds of people in this country: those in prison and those guarding them. If we legalize drugs today, tomorrow not one drug lord or terrorist could make a penny from selling drugs.

### Shouldn't we at least try to eliminate drugs from our society?

There has never been and never will be a drug-free society. The War on Drugs is a vicious cycle costing us more and more each year and overburdening the criminal justice system, all with an impossible goal of eliminating drugs from society. Our valuable resources should be focused on a different goal: drug policies that encompass reason, compassion, and justice while reducing harms associated with drug use and misuse.

**But drug usage rates are falling. That means our policies are working, right?**

No. Historically, drug use rates tend to fluctuate over time, often with little relationship to our nation's punitive policies. Instead of celebrating a few percentage points, let's measure the success of our policies based on the problems we most have to worry about-the death, the disease, the crime, and the suffering associated both with drug abuse and with our drug policies. Such a measurement would reflect the true impact of drug abuse and drug policies on our communities and reveal more practical solutions.

**Is it true that current drug policies unfairly target minorities?**

Yes. Despite the fact that drug use rates are more or less consistent across racial lines, many punitive drug laws and enforcement practices unfairly target minorities. Although African Americans represent less than one in seven drug users, they are charged with more than a third of drug offenses and comprise a shocking 59% of those convicted of such offenses, African Americans are also sentenced to larger prison terms than other groups.

**Doesn't drug policy reform send the wrong message to children?**

No. Drug policy reform teaches kids how to focus on creating a constructive society rather than a punitive one. American teenagers in the 1990s had more drug education than any generation in history, but the simplistic "just say no" message did not make them safer from the death, disease, crime, and suffering associated with drug abuse and drug policies. When it comes to young people, let's work on sending them the right message: safety first. While we hope that youth will choose not to use drugs, we need to focus on preventing teens who do experiment from falling into abusive patterns, and we need to create fallback strategies that protect them from harm. Putting safety first requires that we provide teens with credible, science-based information about drugs. Teens will make smart choices when given accurate, honest information.

About 36% of new AIDS cases and hepatitis and other infectious diseases in the US are linked to injected drug use. To cope with the problem, syringe exchange is available in many progressive communities.

Like Canada, treatment via public health departments, instead of prison for addicts, is occurring widely in the US. Methadone and other agents are used. California, Wisconsin, and Alabama have pioneered in these drug abuse programs.

Methamphetamine and Ecstasy are the newest illicit drugs on the US scene. Meth use is said to be an epidemic. It's been called America's most dangerous drug. About 5% of Americans have tried it, and along with cocaine and heroin, it's probably the most commonly used illegal drug in the US. While it's available by prescription for sleep disorders, it's been estimated that about 20% comes from small-scale domestic labs using cold meds and other household materials. Consequently, the sale of cold and allergy meds has been restricted. But the gap has been filled by Mexican cartels.

As a result of the Bush Administration's effort, school drug testing of high school students is now commonplace. But evidence from random testing of 75,000 students in 700 high schools failed to show any more deterrence from drug use than schools that didn't test.

The US-financed coca eradication in South America has been a vicious and inhumane undertaking. Bolivia, the continent's poorest nation, has suffered immensely. The coca leaf is a locally grown crop, of sacred rituals, of a way of life that allowed Bolivia's peasants, by chewing on the bitter leaves that give energy and stave off hunger, to endure the harsh, cold conditions in the high silver and tin mines, where they worked as slaves for the Spaniards for some 300 years, and where many still labor under perilous conditions. As indigenous culture increasingly becomes a mark of pride in Bolivia and across the continent, the symbol of the coca leaf has gained even more importance, and the US war against it has caused increased animosity toward Americans.

Since 2000 the US has poured more than $4 billion dollars into Plan Columbia, a program that has provided everything from police training to Black Hawk Helicopters to a nation that supplies 90% of the cocaine and much of the heroin used in the US. Officials say that intensive fumigation of crops has reduced cocaine production, has caused a squeeze in supplies, and a jump in the price of the drug in the US. And a record number of Colombian traffickers have been extradited to the US for trial. But, in spite of Plan Colombia, the drugs are just as available as ever. Colombia's president, Alvaro Uribe, as opposed to coca farmers who must find other places to grow their crops after their farms have been sprayed, likes Plan Colombia. It helps his troops keep their guerilla adversaries, who depend on illegal drug sales to finance their operations, at bay.

Like Colombia and Bolivia, Afghanistan, which supplies 90% of the world's heroin, is also the victim of the US war on drugs. So far, US efforts have not been very successful.

Finally, believe it or not, the US war on drugs is having an impact on American doctors and their patients. Many physicians are nervous about prescribing pain relieving narcotics for their patients, miserable because of pain, and there are over 30 million of them suffering from chronic pain, causing diseases and disorders. More than 5,600 docs have been investigated in the past few years, and several have been prosecuted, and at least one imprisoned. The DEA has more than $150 million to harass and prosecute doctors and their desperately sick patients battling chronic conditions.

In conclusion, it cannot be denied that the US war on drugs has become an evil, irrational, outrageous affront to our core beliefs that people should not be punished for what they do to, or put into their own bodies, absent harm to others!!

It is a very slow process but momentum is gradually bringing the US, like many EU nations, toward a rational acceptance of unrestricted drug use. And when we finally get there, we should face the reality that most young people will try taking this or that drug on their own, and occasionally end up in tragedy. Since we know it's going to happen, we should be prepared and set up supervising organizations, such as drug camps, to allow young people to sign up for a weekend or more, experimenting under mature, expert, experienced professionals. Will we eventually acquire the wisdom to create such a beneficial undertaking? Let's hope so.

## THE DEATH PENALTY

The first European nation to abolish the death penalty was the Netherlands in 1870. All the others have followed suit. The first US state to do so was Michigan in 1848. Since then, a dozen more states have done away with the death penalty, and most of the others have effective habitual offender laws, which keep the most likely capital offenders off the streets.

Today, 37 of the 38 states with death penalty laws allow juries to consider life without parole an option. Consequently, there are more than 3300 people on death row, and in 2004 California had the most with 637. Along with Texas and

Florida, these 3 states had 44% of the nation's death row populations.

In 2004 12 states executed 59 inmates. Of these, Texas accounted for 23.

36 were white, 19 black, and 3 Hispanic. Two states suspended the death penalty to DNA evidence showing the accused person's innocence. More than half of the countries in the world have abolished the death penalty, but not the US!! We execute more men and women than any country in the world except China, Iran, and Vietnam.

Prior to the recent Supreme Court decision ending the practice, the United States was only one of six countries in the world in which the juvenile death penalty was lawful. The United States has been responsible for two-thirds of the juvenile executions worldwide since 2002. The juvenile death penalty remains in force in China, the Democratic Republic of Congo, Iran, Nigeria, and Saudi Arabia.

The UN Commission on Human Rights has called upon all nations not to execute a person suffering from any form of mental disorder. The US response has been to ignore this resolution. The US Supreme Court upheld the execution of those with mental retardation in 1987, but said it should be a mitigating factor.

At least 34 individuals identified with mental retardation have been executed since 1976 (about 6% of all US executions), though not everyone is tested. 27%

Of death row inmates were determined to have potential mental retardation. The

US Department of Justice says that 1% of prison inmates

suffer from mental illness.

## Minor Lifers

Until the Supreme Court ruled the practice cruel and unusual punishment, America was the only country that executed murderers who committed their

Offenses when they were under 18. We tend to forget that the United States is also one of a small minority of nations that permit life-without-parole sentences for child offenders. According to a joint report by Human Rights Watch and Amnesty International, 2,225 youths who committed a crime while they were minors are currently spending the rest of their lives in US prisons without hope of parole. Of this number—by far the highest in the world—93 percent were convicted of murder, 26 percent of those for felony murder, i.e., as accessories to crimes involving murder. More statistics: 59 percent of those sentenced were first offenders, forty-two states allow such sentences, blacks are ten times more likely than whites to receive them. Thirteen other nations permit LWOP for convicted minors, 132 specifically ban it. There are only about twelve LWOP child offenders in the rest of the world.

The U.S. military has its own death penalty statute, utilizing lethal injection, though no executions have been carried out in over thirty years.

According to the U.S. Department of Justice, 2, 135, 901 prisoners are currently being held in federal, state, or local prisons in the U.S.- twice as many as in Russia and about 25 percent more than in China. This number represents 486 inmates per 100,000 U.S. residents, an increase from 411 in 1995. Although crime rates are decreasing, courts continue to put more people- at an ever-increasing cost-in jail.

Attitudes are slowly changing. At its peak, 80 percent of

people in the U.S. supported the death penalty. Today this has eroded to 64 percent, still a majority.

Support for the death penalty continues to come from the GOP and the White House. On December 2 President Bush reiterated his strong support for the death penalty. Bush, while governor of Texas, oversaw 152 executions, more than any other governor in recent history, and commuted only one. He okayed the execution of a 33-year-old prisoner with the communication skills of a 7-year-old and the first woman executed in Texas in more than 100 years. Publicly, Bush said he sought "guidance through prayer" – that must have been before becoming a "compassionate conservative."

Deterrence, the most often stated argument for the death penalty, is highly questionable. According to the FBI Preliminary Uniform Crime Report, the murder rate in the South increased by 2.1 percent in 2002 while the South has accounted for 82 percent of all executions since 1976.

Researchers examined executions between 1984 and 1997, and concluded that the number of executions was unrelated to murder rates in general and that the number of executions was also unrelated to felony rates.

Another argument, based on purely economic issues, is the "I don't want to pay for their oatmeal" position towards those on death row. There is no evidence to back up this argument either. A New Jersey Policy Perspectives report, commissioned by New Jerseyans for Alternatives to the Death Penalty, found that convicting a killer and putting him or her to death costs about four times more than imprisoning him for life without parole. An Illinois State University study estimated that the death penalty process has cost New Jersey tax payers $253 million since 1983. Studies by the Death Penalty Information Center found that the cost of capital trials far exceeds the cost of other types of trials.

Of course there's an argument that those sentenced to death should only get one appeal, but this perspective overlooks the 172 exonerations of innocent people-including 14 people who were at one time sentenced to death- that the Innocence Project has won.

Today one in twenty men can expect to spend part of his life in prison. And an exploding prison population means nearly 5 million are unable to vote because they have been convicted of a felony-defined as any crime that carries a sentence of a year or more in prison. Today felons and former felons are the single largest group currently barred by law from voting in the United States.

Voting rights are left up to the states, so the laws vary. Only Maine and Vermont allow prisoners to vote. Most states take the right away from those in prison and also those on parole or probation. While most states also return the right to vote once the terms of a sentence have been completed, thirteen states, five of them In the South, take voting rights away for life-a punishment extremely rare in the rest of the Western world. As a result, there are now more ex-prisoners than prisoners in the United States who can't vote.

Many states passed disenfranchisement laws in the years after Reconstruction, when blacks were first gaining the right to vote. At the time lawmakers justified the laws by invoking what one Alabama politician called the "menace of negro domination." This was at the exact same historical period when poll taxes and literary requirements were being adopted by many Southern legislatures." "All with the express purpose of disenfranchising black voters, so that one Southern legislator at the time referred to the felon disenfranchisement laws as almost an insurance policy." Today the laws are justified on race-neutral grounds, but their discriminatory impact remains.

Also, American laws seem to be out of sync with those of other countries in their severity. Prisoners never lose their right to vote in eighteen countries across Europe- including Ireland, Spain, Switzerland and Poland. In South Africa, Prisoners helped to elect one of their own—Nelson Mandela. And last year the

Supreme Court of Canada ruled that denying prisoners the vote is "anti-democratic" and '" denies the basis of democratic legitimacy."

In the United States the laws affect large numbers of people, and black people in particular. Across the country, one in eight African-American men is barred from voting. In Florida and Alabama, it's one in tree. Sometimes felon disenfranchisement laws take the vote away from whole communities. In New York State, 90 percent of prisoners serve their time upstate, yet overwhelmingly these prisoners come from just seven poor, minority neighborhoods in New York City.

A poll taken last year showed that 80 percent of Americans support restoring the vote to ex-felons who have completed their sentences. "I don't want these people having access to making changes in my life," says Janice Grieshaber, whose daughter Jenna was murdered in Albany in 1997, one week before she was to graduate from nursing school. Grieshhaber says it's really pretty simple: People who don't follow the rules shouldn't have a say in making them.

Yet even Grieshaber makes a distinction between the rights of violent and nonviolent criminals. As she sees it, someone locked up because of drugs or a white-collar crime is a more sympathetic figure than, say, someone convicted of manslaughter. And some politicians and criminologists agree. Chris Uggan, a sociologist at the University of Minnesota who studies felon disenfranchisement, says that those fighting for felons' right to vote would have a better chance of success if they focused on nonviolent criminals.

But if history offers any lessons, it won't be an easy

fight or a quick one. That's because, according to some sociologists who study disenfranchisement, The removal of barriers for felons could affect the political balance of power in this country. For one thing, felons who get the chance vote overwhelmingly Democratic, and with a Republican administration in power, there is little chance for change on a national scale.

Chris Uggan found that had felons been allowed to vote in the last presidential election, hanging chads would have never been an issue. Uggan looked at the closely contested 2000 election and discovered that had felons had the vote, Al Gore would have likely won the popular vote by more than a million votes. In Florida alone, Gore would have picked up 60,000-80,000 votes—enough to swamp the narrow victory margin declared by George Bush.

Judges in several states have started to put up potentially insurmountable roadblocks to the use of legal injections to execute condemned inmates. Their doctors take an active role in supervising executions, even though the

American Medical Association's code of ethics prohibits that. The recent decisions, by contrast, rely on accounts of witnesses, post-mortem testing, and execution logs that seem to show that executions meant to be humane have, in fact, caused excruciating pain.

The method of execution is by firing squad in Utah. The other states administer lethal injection of three chemicals. 1st: Sodium Thiopental, a short acting barbituate, which produces sleep; 2nd: pancuronium, a relative of curare, causing paralysis; and 3rd: potassium heart chloride, which stops the heart. If given improperly, it would cause agonizing pain. Accordingly, the "executioner" should be good at getting the needle securely into the vein, and it may be difficult. But many lab techs, nurses, and doctors are experts. Their skills should be utilized. But many doctors refuse, citing the AMA ethics code against causing death. In veterinary euthanasia and in assisted suicides in Oregon, a single lethal dose of a long-acting barbituate is typically used.

But corrections officials and their medical experts say using that method in executions would take too long and would subject witnesses to discomfort.

The A.M.A. can't do much to censure physicians who decide on their own to participate in executions. And almost all doctors involved in executions take great pains to conceal their identity—from hiding during the execution to requesting payment in cash so there's no check to trace back to the state. When doctors do admit to having helped the state execute an inmate, activists are there to make their life difficult. An ethical grievance filed by a Georgia doctor was eventually dismissed, but it did inspire the Georgia house of representatives to pass legislation in February that would protect the medical license of any doctor who participates in executions. A similar grievance filed by Zitrin and others against Kentucky Governor Ernie Fletcher, a licensed doctor who signed his first death warrant in November 2004, also failed, but Zitrin is unbowed. " Doctors should not be handmaidens to executioners," he says. "We have a responsibility to maintain life as long as there is a possibility to do so."

But other doctors quibble with that interpretation of the Hippocratic oath. In a certain light, a condemned prisoner whose death is imminent and assured could be viewed as a terminal patient. Then the doctor's palliative presence through the dying process takes on a nobler tone. Despite he A.M.A.'S objections, a survey published in 2000 by the Archives of Internal Medicine found that 43% of responding physicians felt it was acceptable for other doctors to inject lethal drugs as part of an execution.

In 1998, the world celebrated the 50th anniversary of the Universal Declaration of Human Rights. This pivotal U.N. document, which the United States helped forge, is being used to limit or abolish the death penalty in regional treaties, and in the decisions of international courts. But precisely at a time when the U.S. needs international cooperation, it is increasingly becoming the target of international criticism for violating the spirit of this document. Our violation of international norms is a source of confusion to our allies, and an excuse for other countries to break other rules of international law. Hiding behind the technicalities of reservations and procedural barriers defies the essence of these treaties and serves us poorly as a leader in the pursuit of human rights into the 21st Century.

Our practices of executing the mentally ill, of refusing to pass legislation to counter racial discrimination in the death penalty, of failing to inform defendants of their consular rights, of increasing executions, and expanding it to new states and new crimes, will mean further isolation of the U.S. from the international community. Unless steps are taken soon to rectify this affront to the norms of international justice, the U.S. will suffer enormously in the critical arena of human rights.

The U.S. is paying an enormous price in obstinately holding onto the death penalty. It has defied consecutive unanimous rulings from the highest international court; it has isolated itself on two of the most important treaties of the century; and it has alienated its allies by turning a deaf ear to their entreaties for mercy and due process; and it has endangered its own citizens abroad by disrespecting international law.

## THE CUBAN EMBARGO

It's no secret that our government's many attempts to oust Fidel Castro by blockading trade with Cuba is one of our nation's greatest policy failures. The U.S. trade embargo has been in place for over 40 years. George W. Bush is now the 10th U.S. President in office since it began. Despite its failure, we still pursue this cruel policy and the misery it brings to Cuban citizens.

Americans are being arrested for going there. Other countries are profiting from trade with Cuba; that trade could go to the U.S. Why haven't we repealed the embargo? Because there is a large number of right wing Cuban Americans opposed to it, and they supported Bush, enabling him to beat Al Gore for President in 2002. And he threatened to veto any move to end the embargo. Yuck!!!!

Widespread support for an end to the embargo has given President Bush all the political cover he needed to finally end the embargo—and what does he do? He not only refuses to loosen the embargo, but actually decided to tighten it. Bush instructed the Treasury Department to prosecute some of the tens of thousands of Americans who have visited Cuba to see it for themselves.

A Seattle man was fined because he went to Cuba to bury the ashes of his parents near the church they had built as missionaries. A 75-year-old retired teacher from Wisconsin was fined $ 7,500 for a cycling trip to Cuba, It sounds like the McCarthy era of the 1950s, but it is happening now.

Bush allows free trade with Middle Eastern and African countries far worse than Cuba on human rights, and of course, with China, which holds political prisoners, forbids freedom of speech or religion, and forbids opposition parties, does not allow elections, and keeps out most human rights monitors.

Opposition to the embargo is growing. Large agricultural corporations, like Archer Daniels Midland, Cargill, and Farmland Industries, recognize that Cuba is a potential market for their products. They want to do business there, and they now support anti-embargo efforts. The American Farm Bureau, and remarkably, the conservative U.S. Chamber of

Commerce, also openly and vigorously oppose the embargo.

Former President Jimmy Carter has spoken out against the embargo. He visited Cuba, the first former or sitting President to do so since Calvin Coolidge in 1928, and upon his return said, " I think an American citizen or an American company should have the right to visit any place on earth and the right to trade with any other purchaser or supplier on earth."

Thanks to this growing opposition to the trade embargo, the U.S. House of Representatives and the U.S. Senate have both passed legislation in the past six months to end the Cuba travel ban. However, even this small step was too much for George Bush. He threatened to veto the entire Treasury appropriations bill, to which the travel ban legislation was attached. To save him that embarrassment, the Republican leadership managed to delete the repeal of the travel ban before the bill came to a vote.

## GUN LAWS

The firearm mortality rate in the US is incredible, unbelievable! According to a 1998 study by the National Center for Health Statistics, in a comparison of 11 industrial nations, the US had an overall firearm death rate of 13.7 per 100,000, which was more than twice as high as France (6.3/100,000). Canada had 3.9 and England/Wales 0.4 (see chart below). For homicide alone, the US rate was over 8 times higher than Israel (the next highest) and over 11 times higher than Canada.

One American youth is killed every hour by gunfire. Since 1994 background check laws have prohibited more than 1,300,000 purchasers from buying firearms. And firearm deaths have dropped from 40,000 to 30,000 every year. About 1500 children are hurt by guns every year, and in 1996, 140 children died after being accidentally shot.

There are about 228,000,000 firearms in the US, as estimated 85 million gun owners, 50 % of whom own handguns. 40% of homes have guns. A flourishing market in illegal guns fueled more than 3,700,000 violent crimes committed with firearms in the past decade.

Ask any group of police officers the one thing that could help prevent all this violence and they will tell you, " Get guns off the streets. And keep guns out of the hands of people who should not have them in the first place!"

## FIREARM MORTALITY RATES IN 11 COUNTRIES (Per 100,000)

| Country | Overall rate | Homicide rate | Suicide Rate | 15-24 DR | Elderly DR |
|---|---|---|---|---|---|
| Australia | 2.9 | 0.4 | 2.3 | 3.7 | 3.6 |
| Canada | 3.9 | 0.5 | 3.2 | 5.0 | 4.3 |
| Denmark | 2.1 | 0.3 | 1.7 | * | * |
| England/Wales | 0.4 | 0.1 | 0.3 | 0.4 | 0.4 |
| France | 6.3 | 0.4 | 5.1 | 4.8 | 9.3 |
| Israel | 2.8 | 0.7 | 1.4 | 5.8 | 2.6 |
| Netherlands | 0.5 | 0.4 | ** | ** | ** |
| New Zealand | 3.1 | 0.4 | 2.3 | 4.4 | 3.6 |
| Norway | 4.3 | 0.3 | 3.9 | 6.6 | 4.1 |
| Scotland | 0.6 | 0.1 | 0.4 | 0.9 | 0.4 |
| U.S. | 13.7 | 5.9 | 7.0 | 27.2 | 14.2 |

*Data not available
*Based on fewer than 20 deaths

Controversial Gun laws are lobbied in Congress and the state legislatures mainly by 3 organizations. In general, the

National Rifle Association and Gun Owners of America are for less restrictive control laws and the Brady Campaign to Prevent Gun Violence for more control. Large sums of money are raised and spent yearly by the 3 groups to influence politicians.

James Brady was President Reagan's news secretary, and in 1981, was shot in the head by a bullet meant for Reagan, from the handgun of the mentally deranged man John Hinckley, which left Brady paralyzed. Subsequently, he and his wife Sarah founded the lobbying group that bears his name. NRA was made famous by its president, the movie actor Charlton Heston.

There are several laws at issue. In the background is the 2$^{nd}$ Amendment to the Constitution, which states: "A well regulated militia, being necessary to the security of a free state, the right of the people to keep and bear arms shall not be infringed." The Supreme Court has held that the right to bear arms doesn't mean that Congress can't prohibit certain kinds of guns that aren't necessary for the common defense.

Most importantly is whether handguns should be banned. Doing so would be an uphill battle because most Americans seem to favor them. The next most controversial issue is the assault weapons ban, which applies to 19 specific models of semi-automatic firearms, and to other guns with assault weapons features. This was passed and signed by President Clinton, and went into effect in May 1994 It expired in 2004, and has not been re-enacted because of strong opposition by gun rights groups.

Other major bills at issue are the Fifty Caliber Sniper, and the Terrorist Apprehension and Record Retention Acts. Other less important bills: Guns in the workplace; Background checks at gun shows; Shoot First Law; Terrorist Watch List; Gun industry above the law; Assault weapons back on the streets; Pediatricians asking if there's a gun in the home; and Right to carry concealed weapons.

Solution:

The present US problem of gun violence has gotten so out-of-hand, so serious, so horrific and outrageous that giant steps must be taken to bring relief.

1. Like the UK, the Netherlands, Canada, and other industrialized countries, the US must make the possession of all handguns and handgun ammo, except for the military, police, licensed security guards, licensed sporting clubs, and licensed gun collectors, totally illegal, with strong, aggressive, thorough enforcement applied. Our philosophy should be: The only reason for guns in civilian hands is for sporting purposes. To reassure those who would feel defenseless and vulnerable if they can't have a handgun, they should be advised to purchase a shotgun or hunting rifle to be kept closely in a bedroom closet, under the bed, or near the front door. It could be carried in a car. And women should be taught how to use the gun safely and expertly. The safety lever should be kept in the "on" position and then out of the hands of children. Nothing is more tragic than when a little boy kills his best friend playing with a gun he found in his father's closet.

2. Ban the importation, manufacture, and sale of handguns, semiautomatic assault weapons, and .50 calibre sniper rifles to private individuals. If the effort to ban these weapons fails, they should at least have trigger locks to prevent tragedy if they should fall into the hands of children.

3. Anyone wanting to own a shotgun or hunting type

rifle, as in the Netherlands, must register it, have a weapons permit certifying no criminal Convictions, and join a government shooting club that monitor his law abiding conduct. And committing a crime would be grounds for dismissal and loss of his weapons permit.

4. End gun sales to individuals on the terrorist watch list and close the lethal " gun show loophole" by requiring and extending the background check time to at least 3 days to cover weekends.

5. Prevent reckless gun dealers from supplying criminals, juveniles, and the mentally ill with guns.

6. Require background checks to be kept at least 90 days.

7. Require testing for mental illness if background checks are suspicious.

8. Limit gun sales to one per month to curb gun traffickers.

9. Implement tougher manufacture standards for gun makers, like child safety locks and technologies that make it easier to trace firearms used in a crime.

10. Outlaw cop-killer bullets that can be fired through police body armor and other protective equipment.

## EUTHANASIA

Every doctor's foremost obsession should be compassion. No law or temptation should be allowed to supercede that motivation. Any doctor that allows anything to overrule his compassion should not be in the practice of medicine. The mandate is especially relevant when it comes to action concerning patients wanting to die because of suffering from incurable diseases. In other words, via physician assisted suicide.

Many US doctors, perhaps most, will go ahead and furnish or prescribe or furnish enough medication to accomplish this. Especially, if the patient can administer it to himself, either orally, or by injection. Many patients don't need a doctor's assistance to end their lives painlessly, Breathing carbon monoxide from their car's exhaust is often used. Some get bottles of insulin, needles and syringes, available without prescription fro all drug stores, to inject into themselves and pass away, calmly and painlessly.

Dr. Jack Kevorkian, many years ago, heroically pioneered assisted suicide, publicly, and was shamefully prosecuted and imprisoned for it. But his courage and dedication to compassion is remembered, and revered by many as a shining example for all doctors to live by.

In 1994 and in 1997, the state of Oregon adopted voter ratified physician-assisted suicide, and in spite of the fact that the Bush administration short- sightedly and disgracefully opposed it, the law passed the Supreme Court by a vote of 6 to 3 in 2006. That means the administration tried to use a federal drug law to prosecute Oregon doctors who prescribed overdoses. The then-Attorney General John Ashcroft incredibly said doctor-assisted suicide is not a "legitimate Medical purpose."

Justices have dealt with end-of-life cases before. In 1990, the Supreme Court ruled that terminally ill people may refuse treatment that would keep them alive. Then, justices in 1997 unanimously ruled that people have no constitutional right to die, upholding state bans on physician-assisted suicide. That opinion by then-Chief Justice William H. Rehnquist, said that individual states could decide to allow the practice.

Oregon's law is called Death with Dignity Act. It requires that 2 doctors Certify that that the patient has no more than 6 months to live. Patients must make 3 requests to the doctor for a lethal dose of medication—twice orally and once in writing. The prescription must be filled only after a 15-day waiting period. The patients must take the drug themselves. Most deaths take place at home with family and a health care worker present.

The Oregon case is a very satisfactory solution to the physician-assisted question. That being, it's strictly up to individualstates,notthefederalgovernment,todecidewhether or not to follow Oregon's example. And many progressive-minded states, such as California, will undoubtedly do so. But not the states where the religious right prevail. In these states, physicians will have to continue following their own consciences regarding end-of-life decisions, with the supreme law of compassion forcing many of them to break the state governments' cruel, unfeeling laws.

In several EU nations, including the Netherlands, Belgium, and Switzerland, euthanasia is legal. In the Netherlands, with the parents' permission, it is also used on severely deformed or terminally ill newborns. Someday, this will hopefully, become legal in the US.

All adults need to compose advance directives, living wills, and health care power of attorneys. The power of attorney is the most important of these because it authorizes someone, like a spouse, relative or friend, to communicate your wishes in case you have lost the power to do so yourself. For instance, Many people don't want to be put on a ventilator in case of respiratory failure, or don't want to be autopsied in case they die, or be kept alive by means of IV or parenteral nutrition, etc. The person given power of authority has legal powers to enforce these wishes.

An advance directive is a written document to make your wishes known in a health care setting. A living will is one type of advance directive coming into effect only after you have been diagnosed as terminally ill.

These measures are especially appropriate for patients in a persistent vegetative state, as was Terri Schiavo . Or those with advanced Alzheimer's Disease, where billions of dollars are spent keeping them alive, instead of being spent on all kinds of merciful causes.

## THE FLAWED US ELECTION PROCESS

In the 2000 presidential election, Vice President Al Gore received 543, 816 more popular votes than Bush, yet he did not become President!! How come? Because the US has a crazy Constitution-based institution called the Electoral College, whereby each state has the number of electoral votes, based on population size of that state, all of which are cast for the candidate receiving the most popular votes.

This is the first time since 1886 that a candidate, who did not receive a plurality vote, received a majority of the Electoral

College. In 1888 Grover Cleveland beat Benjamin Harrison by about 100,000 votes but lost the Electoral College by 233 to 168. In 1892, Cleveland beat Harrison to become the first President to serve 2 non-consecutive terms.

### Origins Of The Electoral College

Members of the Constitutional Convention explored many possible methods of choosing a president. One suggestion was to have the Congress choose the president.

A second suggestion was to have the state legislatures select the president. A third suggestion was to elect the president by a direct popular vote. The first suggestion was voted down due to suspicion of corruption, fears of irrevocably dividing the Congress, and concerns of upsetting the balance of power between the executive and the legislative branches. The second idea was voted down because the Framers felt that federal authority would be compromised in exchange for votes. And the third idea was rejected out of concern that the voters would only select candidates from their state without adequate information about candidates outside of the state. The prevailing suggestion was to have a College of Electors select a president through an indirect election.

The College of Electors was likened to the Centurial Assembly of the Roman Republic, where adult male citizens of Rome were divided into groups of 100 who cast one in favor or against proposals of the Roman Republic. In the Electoral College system, the states would assume the role of a centurial group, and the number of votes that they are entitled to depend on the size of the state's Congressional delegation. Originally, the purpose of the College of Electors was to have the most knowledgeable and informed individuals from each state of the Union cast their votes for the president, assuming that they voted solely on the basis of merit.

Throughout its history, the Electoral College has gone through only two major changes. In the first design of the Electoral College:

•Each state's Electors numbered their two U.S. Senators(2) plus its Representatives.

•The states selected the manner in which their Electors were chosen;

• However, members of Congress and federal employees were prohibited from serving as Electors.

• Electors were required to meet in their states.

• Each elector was required to cast two votes for the president, and at least one of those votes had to be a candidate outside of their state.

• The candidate with the most electoral votes became president, and the candidate with the next greatest number of electoral votes became vice president.

This system was meant to work in a system without political parties and national campaigns and the introduction of which forced a couple features of the Electoral College to change.

The second design of the Electoral College came about in the presidential election of 1800 when the Electors of the Democratic-Republican Party gave Thomas Jefferson and Aaron Burr an equal number of electoral votes. The tie breaking decision was made in the House of Representatives , which resulted in the election of Thomas Jefferson. To prevent a tie from occurring again, the 12th Amendment was passed, requiring each elector to cast only one vote for the office of president and another for the office of vice president. The 12th Amendment also states that if no one receives an absolute majority of electoral votes for president, the House of Representatives will cast the deciding vote from the three top candidates.

The Electoral College's raison d'etre was never accomplished. It did not prevent the 2-party system from developing.

Nor did it give smaller states more power. Its biggest deficiency, as we have seen, is that it does not guarantee that the office will go to the most popular candidate. A second major negative factor is that it may depress voter turnout because a state gets so many electoral votes regardless of the number of popular voters going to the polls. And the U.S. is the only nation having such a system, which shows that it's generally considered not useful.

To eliminate the Electoral College would require amending the Constitution, which is a fairly onerous task. But, since most polls show that Americans want the president to be elected by popular vote, it's one that should be tackled. Short of that, a solution has been suggested that each state gives all its electoral votes to the popular winner, and since this is a process the constitution leaves up to the state to decide, this proposal would work. But it would add to the world's opinion that we are poor at solving problems.

## Instant Runoff Voting

In our flawed present system of US voting, a candidate in a field of three may win, even though he or she is unacceptable to most voters, simply because the majority split their vote among a combination of other acceptable candidates. This is alleged to have happened in a recent US presidential election, when a Green Party candidate drew votes away from the Democrat, which caused him to lose to the Republican. The Green Party candidate became known as 'the Spoiler".

How does instant runoff voting work?

Voters simply rank the candidates and mark their ballots with Their first choice, second choice, etc. Ballots are counted by first choices to see if there is a majority winner. If not, a runoff election is counted by " eliminating" the last place candidate, and transferring each ballot cast for him/her to the remaining contenders, based on the voter's ranking. If this doesn't produce a majority winner, the process is repeated until it does.

## This System Has Several Benefits Including:

(1) Nobody's vote will be wasted because of supporters of third-party, independent, or underdog candidates will not feel compelled to vote for a less favorable front-runner for fear of throwing the election to a decidedly unacceptable candidate. Voters will therefore be able to vote their true beliefs with their first-choice votes, while still making effective back-up choices among the remaining acceptable candidates.

(2)The taxpayers and candidates will save money because primary elections become unnecessary.

(3)Successful candidates will reflect more closely the will of the people and a clearer mandate for a winning candidate's position will be created, giving better direction for policy making.

(4) Positive, issue-based campaigns will be encouraged, and negative campaigning will be significantly reduced because candidates will have to appeal to a broader audience in order to attract second and third choice votes.

(5) Losing candidates, who offered programs acceptable to some of the voters, will not forever be tagged as "spoilers" or the "candidate who elect the candidate of the opposing party."

(6) Voter interest and turnout should increase because a voter has more choices, and all votes will be more meaningful than under the present system.

## Campaign Finance Reform

An election reform that is long overdue is requiring elections to be publicly funded and banning " legalized bribery" by lobbyists, large donors, and wealthy special interests. Some commentators joke that "Congress really isn't for sale because the current owners are quite pleased with it." However, Congress has been very negligent about addressing this issue. Yet, it has been turning the public's stomach for a long time.

Meanwhile, several states have passed public funding of elections. Broadcasters should be required to provide free or reduced cost TV and radio ads for candidates.

Finally, lobbyist corruption has become a big issue and legal reform is taking place.

## Chaos and Corruption at the Polls

Both the 2000 and the 2004 presidential elections saw shameful things going on. The presidential vote in Florida in 2000 was marred voting machine issues like rejected ballots, "hanging chads", and the possibly confusing "butterfly ballot." The vote count between Bush and Gore was so questionable, and there being no paper trail, the US Supreme Court finally stepped in and declared Bush the winner.

In 2004, corruption occurred in Ohio, when an electronic voting system gave Bush 4,256 votes when only 638 votes were cast. In North Carolina thousands of votes were lost when a computer ran out of disk space.

Across the country, the electoral process was riddled with problems. For instance, some voters waited in line for up to 10 hours to cast a ballot. And thousands were turned away from the polls. And "official" fliers directed people to the wrong polling places.

Touch screen voting machines rely on computers to count votes, but there's no hard copy backup in case of a crash and no way to detect tampering. The answer is paper records so that votes can be counted. In addition to these measures, voter ID should be tightened up re citizenship, legal name registration, ballot by mail, etc. using voter and signature verification.

## Sunday Voting

All EU nations and many other countries vote on Sundays, which helps working people get to the polls without missing work. And close to one half of Americans don't vote. Our constitution makes Tuesday official voting day but more Americans would undoubtedly vote if it were Sunday, instead. Therefore, we should amend our constitution in this regard.

### Felon Voting

Once a felon has paid his debt to society, he should be allowed to vote, the way it is in most EU countries.

If the American people wre judged by the quality of their election system, they should be deeply ashamed of themselves. In fact, a study by political scientists and former politicians found that our nation's electoral system is the weakest in North America. Weaker than Canada's, and yes, even weaker than our much-maligned neighbor to the south, Mexico. The challenges we face in reforming our election system are daunting, but we must meet them and conquer them, if our democracy is to be preserved.

## UNIVERSAL GLOBAL LANGUAGE

It is very troubling that a universal language has not been created enabling every human on earth to converse with every other person. With the coming of the internet there is no corner of the world that cannot be instantly gotten in touch with. Why hasn't the UN been assigned the job of canvassing all its members regarding their preferences about this? Should a currently existing language be chosen? Or should a new one with a new alphabet be developed? Whichever, there are many linguistic scholars that could do the job expertly.

Every child on earth should first learn his native language from his parents or family members. Then early in his schooling, start learning the universal global language.

There are good reasons that English be chosen as the universal global language. It is already the language of medicine and science, worldwide, mainly because of the advances made by English speaking doctors and scientists and their numerous organizations and journals.

But a more important reason has recently evolved…. That being the internet with its worldwide adaptation and its English speaking origins. It's amazing how many Chinese are avidly learning English in order to use the internet, and to compete economically. In spite of the fact that their language is native to 3 times as many people as English!

English, in its present form, cannot be expected to appeal as the universal global language because of its chaotic non-phonetic spelling, which badly needs reform. Learning to speak It from a book is almost impossible. It must be heard to be learned, as many foreigners will tell you.

Reform of English spelling has been proposed several times going back to Noah Webster in 1783. He was supported in his effort by his friend Benjamin Franklin, who tried to sell it to America, saying, "Sometime or other it must be done." But he wasn't able to convince his countrymen to go ahead with it. English is not the only language to need spelling reform.

It has been advocated in several other countries with varying success, including France, Germany, Indonesia, Japan, Norway, Portugal, Spain, and Russia. In the late 1800s Esperanto, an artificial language with a vocabulary based on word roots common to many European languages, was developed but never became widely popular.

An international organization named the Simplified Spelling Society was founded in 1908 with the aim of reforming the spelling of English, making it phonetic. If the US government and perhaps the UK and others, under the leadership of this society, proposed to the UN that phonetically spelled English be declared the universal global language, it might be acceptable to the majority of UN members. At least it should be tried. To paraphrase the words of Ben Franklin, "Sometime or other....

And now is the time!"

## OTHER COMMUNICATION PROBLEMS

The US should be addressing other problems that brand us, in the eyes of the world, as regressive dissenters, stubbornly going our own way. High on this list is refusing to switch to the metric system, as the rest of the world has done. We should give up Fahrenheit in favor of Celsius. The former was adopted from the freezing and boiling points of salt water, as found by the German-Dutch physicist Gabriel D. Fahrenheit in 1724. A more sensible scale of zero for freezing and 100 for boiling of pure water was developed also in the early 1700s by Anders Celsius, a Swedish astronomer. The temperature scale is also called centigrade and is universal throughout the world except for the US.

Also, a universal unit except in the US is the metric system and one meter is based on the distance light travels in a given period of time. From that comes centimeter (cm), one hundredthand millimeter (mm), one thousandth of a meter, and cubic centimeter(cc), and liter, one thousand ccs. The unit of weight is the gram, the weight of one cc of water, and the kilogram (kg), the weight of one liter of water.

The US scientific community has switched to Celsius, centigrade, and the metric system, but unfortunately, not the general public. But someday, in the distant future, it will probably happen, as we gradually get in step with the rest of the world.

Another place where we're wrong is calling them Indians instead of native Americans. Columbus made that mistake over 500 years ago. Yet, we've known for most of that time an ocean separates us from India, but we persist. Let's change "Bureau of Indian Affairs" to "Bureau of Native American Affairs," showing respect for our good Asian friends, the real Indians.

Another item we ought to change is to stop calling it "football" because to the rest of the world football is what we call "soccer," and since their football doesn't include punting, throwing passes or tackling we should change our term for it to something like "tackleball".

The English language is needlessly complex with spelling and pronunciation of words that have been modernized or revised. Why is it that we modernize and update all kinds of inventions, appliances, hardware and software, autos and airplanes,, medical procedures and technology, but not our language? How come we don't look at other languages such as Spanish and realize we could communicate so much more  efficiently, if we would simplify English? Is English so sacred that we dare not touch it? After Chinese, which is the most spoken language in the planet (over 1 billion people speaking it).

English is next most common with over 500 million speaking it as their native language, so c'mon, simplifying it, spelling and pronunciation-wise it would not only save time and money… but lives! (airplane crashes,etc.)

## HOMOSEXUALITY

Homosexuality is normal throughout the animal kingdom including homo sapiens. The incidence in human males is between 5 and 10%, and slightly lower for females. Brain imaging studies have shown it to be a physical variant.

Male homosexuals are called gays and females lesbians. A small percentage of both are bisexual.

"Homophobia" is the irrational fear and hatred of homosexuals. People who are homophobic are often afraid to get to know lesbians and gays. They are sometimes afraid that other people will think they are gay or lesbian. Or, they worry that a gay or lesbian person is attracted to them. If they do not know gays or lesbians, they don't realize that these fears are not necessary.

In the US, some organizations and individuals discriminate against homosexuals. For example, school teachers can lose their jobs if someone thinks they are homosexual. Homosexuals can be refused housing or be evicted from their homes. In addition, they are sometimes physically attacked. Homophobia and discrimination against homosexuals exist everywhere in the US.

Every civilization has approved, disapproved or ignored homosexuality throughout history. Laws prohibiting homosexuality were called "sodomy laws," and made sodomy a criminal offense. By 1961, all US states and territories and the military had these laws on their books.

Some were worded so generally that they criminalized consensual oral sex in private between married couples.

England's 1st anti-homosexual law, the '"Buggery Act", was piloted thru Parliament by Thomas Cromwell in 1533. It made homosexual acts punishable by hanging. The 13 colonies adopted it in 1624, and immediately hung a ship captain for committing sodomy with a 29-year-old cabin boy. In 1772 an English sea captain was sentenced to death for sodomizing a 13-year-old boy, the age of consent being 14, but he was pardoned by the King on condition that he leave the country. Much public debate followed and calls made to reform the law, and it was concluded that homosexuals have an "inborn propensity".

Mexican independence from Spain in 1821 brought an end to the Inquisition and homosexual oppression. Adoption of the Napoleonic Code in 1862 in Mexico meant that "sexual conduct in private between adults, whatever their gender, ceased to be a criminal matter."

In 1917 the Soviet Union abolished all anti-gay legislation.

In 1971 Germany outlawed "lewd and unnatural behavior" ,which put a damper on gays. Hitler rose to power in 1932, and at first tolerated gays because he needed their support but later felt threatened by them. He purged them from the army, closed their bars and hotels, sterilized them, and then ordered them put to death or sent to concentration camps along with Jews, gypsies, and other minorities.

In the 1960s US pro-gay and lesbian organizations, thru public demonstrations and legal challenges, much of the government's civil rights  oppression re jobs and dismissals. And some young men tried to stay out of the Vietnam war claiming they were gay.

In 1969 a major riot broke out in Greenwich Village, New York City, when police raided a gay bar. It went on for 2 nights with about 2000 people spraying 400 police with rocks and other projectiles. The founding of the Gay Liberation Front soon followed, and similar organizations were created in many countries Including Canada, France, Britain, Germany, Belgium, the Netherlands, Australia and New Zealand.

In 1977 in San Francisco Harvey Milk was the first openly gay person to be elected to a major post in a large US city. He was later assassinated and became a martyr for the gay community. Now, there are several openly gay members of Congress and local governments. In 1933 the Clinton administration instituted the 'don't ask, don't tell" policy protecting gays in the military. And in 1996 a law allowing states to recognize or deny a marriage or deny a marriage relationship between persons of the same sex. And in 1998 President Clinton signed an executive order banning anti-gay discrimination against any federal employee.

Since the late 1970s significant public controversy has occurred re the Boy Scouts of America excluding homosexuals, agnostics and atheists. In 2005 the Supreme Court ruled that due to these discriminatory policies, the Dept. of Defense could no longer support the National Scout Jamboree. And critics have, in vain, called upon President Bush to step down as honorary president of BSA.

Finally, in 2003 the Supreme Court struck down most states' sodomy laws, and those of the remaining nine states are considered null and void.

## SAME-SEX MARRIAGE

In 2006 President Bush suffered a stunning defeat when the Senate overwhelmingly defeated his constitutional amendment banning gay marriage.

48 Senators including 7 Republicans voted against it and

49 Senators included 2 Democrats voted for it, denying the president the two-thirds majority needed for passage. But, it remains a hot issue in state legislatures and courts.

The issue received a big boost in 2003 when the Massachusetts Supreme Court ruled that a law barring same-sex marriage was inconsistent with the state constitution and was the first state to issue licenses for same-sex marriage.

Vermont and Connecticut had previously been the only states to allow civil union performed for same-sex couples providing the same rights, benefits and responsibilities but not recognizing them as married, but were followed by California, District of Columbia, Hawaii, Maine, and New Jersey.

45 of the 50 states had passed laws and amended their constitutions to prohibit same-sex marriages but several have been rejected by judges including Washington, California and New York. Several municipalities in 2004 wedded same-sex couples, but all have been halted and the marriages voided.

Many other countries including several in the EU, China, Taiwan, Canada, Australia, Iceland and South Africa have legalized same-sex marriages or civil unions.

Even among the 75% of Americans who support gay rights, half are against gay marriage. Why so much controversy over gay marriage? Is it blighting civilization? Is it bringing pain and suffering to millions? Why is it that many people don't want others to have happy lives when they themselves want happy lives? It's gross selfishness!!

Various irrational arguments are used against gay marriage, eg "Marriage is an institution between one man and one woman." or "Same sex couples aren't The optimum environment in which to raise children" or "Gay relationships are Immoral" or "Same sex marriage threatens the institution of marriage" or "Same Sex marriage is an untried social experiment" or "Same sex marriage would start us down the slippery slope towards legalized incest, bestial marriage, polygamy.

And all kinds of other horrible consequences" or "Gay marriages would force churches to marry gay couples when they have a moral objection to doing so" or "Sodomy should be illegal'.

The real reason many people oppose gay marriage is that they're just not comfortable with the idea. And the thought of gay sex is unnatural and repulsive to them.

The attitude of churches toward gay marriage is mixed. Roman Catholic, Islamic, Methodist, Lutheran and Pentecostal are con. Unitarian Universalist, United Church of Christ, and Metropolitan Community Church are pro, and the rest are mixed, some pro and some con.

## PROSTITUTION

Legalization and regulation of the world's oldest profession is now a reality

In the Netherlands, Germany, Denmark, Sweden, France, England, Israel, Australia, Canada, and Nevada. But not the rest of the US. We're still in the dark ages. We're still arresting "sex workers" and their "johns" right and left. And Pimping, sex trafficking, or ignoring the problem is rife.

Most legalized prostitution occurs in brothels, and the "madams" and their employees pay taxes, are covered by some form of social security, are required to be at least 18, and are frequently checked for sexually transmitted diseases (STDs). They are also required to use condoms. Street prostitution is illegal in most countries.

There are many benefits to legalized prostitution including allowing enforcement to respond to more important crimes, freeing justice systems from nuisance cases, helping women who are trapped by prostitution, and preventing teens from being ensnared into it. Countries that don't ban prostitution have less rapes and murders, people in prison, suicides and divorces, and less HIV/ AIDS problems.

## STEM CELL RESEARCH

Stem cell research is moving ahead slowly, using stem cells taken from adult tissues, not embryonic, which is better than nothing. This unfortunate situation happened because President Bush irrationally vows to veto any bill allowing stem cell research, and even the embryos are frozen with no plans to ever use them to create human beings.

Most stem cell researchers think embryonic stem cells have a much greater development potential than adult stem cells. Adult stem cells can renew themselves and repair or duplicate damaged issues from whence they came. New corneas have restored eyesight in persons with untreatable eye damage.

And lab animal research has shown that re-grown nerve cells for paralyzed persons are being developed. New brain neurons for stroke patients, new heart muscle cells for heart disease, new skin cells for burn victims, and a huge array of other diseases and conditions will be treatable.

Stem cells taken from placenta and cord blood are an invaluable resource and have cured infants with leukemia. Cord blood banking is now commonplace.

Embryonic stem cells, which come from the inner cell mass of a human embryo, have the potential to develop in to all or nearly all of the tissues in the body. More than 60 stem cell types have been developed in labs in the US, Australia, Sweden, Israel, and India. Common diseases like diabetes will probably Soon be cured with insulin producing embryonic pancreatic beta cells. And many other common and less common diseases, also, from the corresponding embryonic stem cell type.

Because of the tremendous curative potential, millions of dollars now come from private and public sources in the US, including California, New York, Wisconsin and Illinois to support stem cell research.

Fortunately, most other countries doing stem cell research don't have Bush-style restraints frustrating their efforts.

## US-UN RELATIONS

Ever since its founding right after WWII, unlike the US rejection of the League of Nations 2 decades earlier, Congress and US presidents, with a few exceptions, such as not paying its annual assessment and not signing the land mine protection agreement, have been quite supportive of the UN and its actions and decisions, until the Bush administration, with its unilateralism, came to power in 2000.

Then came many refusals and disagreements.

In December 2000, President Clinton, recognizing the need for an international judicial body to deal with the many heinous war crimes and judicial tyrants in Europe, Africa and Asia, and knowing that US legal actions would only be complemented, not overridden, signed the Rome Treaty, which established the International Criminal Court in the Hague. But just weeks later, the Bush Administration, vowing to do everything in their power to keep the US from joining the ICC, announced they were "unsigning" the treaty—a step no US president had ever taken before. Another very regrettable US action was refusing to sign the Kyoto Protocol on global warming, signed by all other industrialized nations, including Russia, except Australia and the US, requiring emission of greenhouse gases. Too hard on the US economy was the president's reason for not signing. Other UN measures rejected by the US included the Anti-Ballistic Missile Treaty; the Biological and Chemical Weapons Convention; the Small Arms Treaty; the Convention on the Rights of the Child; the Law of the Sea; the Global Fund for AIDS, TB, and Malaria; and the United Nations Population Fund.

Then, after 9/11, the Bush Administration, in spite of the UN's Hans Blix's denial that Saddam possessed weapons of mass destruction and Joseph Wilson's finding no materials for making atomic bombs in Niger, sent Colin Powell, in vain, to the UN for support for invading Iraq.

Finally, in 2006, the US became more cooperative when the US Senate voted to pay its full share of UN peacekeeping costs, raising it from 25% to 27% of the total. These apportionments are based on a country's wealth. (The General Assembly says the US should pay 31%).

At long last, and in spite of the US's past orneriness, there Is reason to be optimistic about the UN's future. Amazingly, the Bush Administration had done a 180 degree turnaround re US-UN Relations and has decided to work with the 192 member nations to bring about the much-needed UN reforms instead of against them.

Out of the darkness of WWII, the UN came as a shining light of hope. But it was given a structure that limited its efficacy at every turn. Instead of an effective standing peacekeeping army militia and police force, the UN has had to scramble—begging and borrowing- to assemble even the most rudimentary peacekeeping force.

Accordingly, the US has proposed 75,000 troops from countries wishing to contribute to peacekeeping missions, Receive training, equipment, and logistical support from the US or other G-8 members. And be available for missions sponsored by the UN, the EU, or the Organization of African States, and the US would put up at least the initial funds—reportedly $660 million.

This action by the US happily surprised and pleased the other UN members, that the US, at least on this occasion, had put away unilateralism, and was not the bully but a needy supplicant. The Bush Administration's past foreign policy had brought a terrible cost in lives, dollars and reputation for America

It was reassuring that the UN was not cowed enough by US bureaucrats to avoid criticizing the US for breaking the UN Convention Against Torture, ratified by the US in 1994, re Abu Ghraib and Guantanamo.

Also being considered is a flaw in the General Assembly, which allows only one vote per nation, whether big or small.

For instance, Tonga's 110,000 people have the same electoral weight as the US with 288, 889, 610 or China with 1,303,775,785.

What is being considered is the weighted vote concept, which would give a nation a number of votes based on population or gross national product or its record on human rights, etc. Another reform would be to take away the veto power of the Security Council, but none of the members would be likely to favor that idea.

A current problem is the composition of the Human Rights Commission. Two of the members are democracies, but three nations, namely Cuba, Saudi Arabia, and Zimbabwe are dictatorships, casting doubt on the panel's credibility.

Also, the secretary general should be given more power to act efficiently.

These are a few of the reforms needing attention and most Americans are very supportive of them. And several US organizations and individuals, including Ted Turner pledging $1 billion, are immensely helpful toward strengthening the UN.

# POLYGAMY

"Life, liberty and the pursuit of happiness"--words expressing ideas Thomas Jefferson and the founding fathers had as part of the underlying motivation for creating a new nation.

It is safe to say that they had in mind it's ok to pursue happiness as long as you hurt no one else in doing so. This includes a great many pursuits that may bring you happiness but are illegal. At least in the US. Polygamy is one of them.

Polygamy has been practiced all over the world and was very common in Biblical times. Solomon, Abraham and Jacob had multiple wives. And it is still common among Arabs and Africans, and not long ago, among Mormons in Utah.

Polygamy has several significant benefits, especially for women. For instance, those trying to juggle careers and motherhood. It can make raising children easier. It provides a more effective choice for a career without devaluing the role of homemaker. And more freedom and expanded horizons than in monogamy. There are two or more to share the housework, the cooking, the childcare, thus freeing each one to have more time to herself to pursue independent goals and objectives. To share work as well as play and grieve and console in times of sadness.

It provides a potential for at least 3 adult incomes and reduces the fear of unemployment. It allows a woman to have a close female friend for life as well as a husband. Being able to marry a man who is already married means that a woman can have a husband who has proved himself, minimizing the risk, and not having to settle for what's left after other women have taken the best pickings.

It lessens the pressure on a man to commit adultery and the scandal and hurt that might accompany it. And since there are more women than men in this world, it offers fulfillment for more females.

Civil unions for 3 consenting adults is a reality in the Netherlands. And Norway and Canada are looking at it. It will undoubtedly happen in the near future in other nations. And next will come single sex unions of 3 or more!

But, unfortunately, not in backward USA, for a long, long time. Message to President Thomas Jefferson, " Sorry Mr. President, but the nation you created and cared so much about, isn't very interested in the third part of your recipe for a healthy nation, " the pursuit of happiness". Better luck next time".

## FAITH BASED RELIGION vs. REASON AND REALITY

Thomas Jefferson, Ben Franklin, Tom Paine and John Adams were deists---that is, they beiieved in one supreme being but rejected revelation and all the supernatural elements of the Christian Church. And John Adams wrote to Jefferson, " this would be the best of all possible worlds, if there were no religions in it". But Franklin and Jefferson believed in the Machiavellian principle that one who aspires to influence the masses must profess religious sentiments and they, like all of the presidents thereafter, at least gave lip service to religion.

They probably would have agreed with the Marxist adage that "religion is the opium of the people."

The US constitution made no mention of God, and the founding fathers fought hard, in Jefferson's words, " to erect a wall of separation of church and state."

### 1st Amendment Violations

"Congress shall make no law respecting the establishment

of religion, " says the 1ˢᵗ Amendment. Then, how come all US money has "In God we trust" on it?

Thomas Jefferson got "E Pluribus Unum" on it in 1782, with no mention of god until 1864, when Congress, beginning to be responsive to the religious community and the votes it was presumed to control, passed the Coinage Act, which designated that in "God we trust appear in place of E Pluribus Unum, on all coins.

It was not until 1955, at the height of cold war tensions, when president Eisenhower signed the bill, that it appeared on all paper money too, simplistically portraying a confrontation between Judeo-Christian civilization and the "godless" menace of communism.

In 1978, the motto was challenged in a US Court of Appeals which invoked the notion of "secular purpose', which suggested that like prayer at government meetings or other displays of religiosity in government, the motto was "really not religious". And that " its use is of a patriotic or ceremonial character and bears no true resemblance to a government sponsorship of a religious exercise" similar to a previous federal court conclusion in 1970.

These arguments may have the ring of truth to some, but are specious, contrived and irrelevant to others. Thomas Jefferson and Benjamin Franklin would turn over in their graves if they were aware of them.

The pledge of Allegiance was composed and adopted in the 1890s by public school officials to be used in flag raising ceremonies. It soon became customary across the nation but it wasn't 'til 1954 that Congress added the words "under god." Now it became a patriotic oath and a public prayer, and it's unlikely that these words will soon be removed from the pledge, since a 2004 case in California was dismissed on a technicality, 3 US Supreme Court justices opined that the expression was simply a "patriotic exercise" as one of them put it, rather than any kind of religious expression.

Other laws mandating public religiosity have been enacted including a statute for all federal justices and judges to swear an oath concluding with"so help me god". And top elected officials take the oath of office swearing on a bible.

Unfortunately, all this government mandated religiosity gives fundamentalist Christians strong assurance that their beliefs are strong and true, and strength and encouragement to persecute and deny civil rights to liberals and progressives.

Prayer and religious activity in public schools has led to much controversy and even violence over the years. For instance, in 1844 in Philadelphia, full-scale riots and bloodshed resulted over which version of the Bible should be used in classroom devotions. And in 1886 in Cincinnati, a "Bible war" divided the city and several people died after the school board discontinued mandatory Bible instruction.

Finally, in 1995 the controversy over prayer and religious activity in public schools subsided when the high court ruled that students may pray or discuss religion among their peers, but public schools are forbidden from sponsoring or pressuring students to pray, meditate, read religious books or take part in religious activities.

The national fuss(furor in some states) over Intelligent Design(creationism) being taught along side evolution took center stage in 2001. At least 43 states have since seen some kind of anti-evolution activity within their borders, the most notorious being Kansas, when in 2005 their Board of Education voted 5-4 approving anti-evolution science teaching in public schools. In the long run, however, the odds of the anti-evolutionists winning, nationally, are not high, in spite of the fact that President George Bush suggested that intelligent design should be taught in the nation's public schools with evolution.

One is reminded of the infamous Scopes Trial, when in 1925 Tennessee made it a crime for any public-school teacher to "teach" any theory that denies the story of divine creation of man" and to " teach instead, that man has descended from a lower of animals". In that same year, John Thomas Scopes was prosecuted by eloquent William Jennings Bryan, defended by Clarence Darrow, and convicted of breaking this law. Later, the Tennessee Supreme Court reversed the conviction on a technicality.

The USA is a very religious society. Evidence abounds demonstrating Americans' deep and abiding religious convictions. A Gallup Poll released in November 2003 found out that six out of ten Americans said that religion was "very important" In their lives.

In contrast, in Canada and the United Kingdom, two societies often perceived as quite similar to the United States, only 28% and 17% respectively described religion as similarly important in their lives.

A survey done in 2001 by the City University of New York Graduate Center found that 85% of Americans identify with some religious faith:

Protestant white evangelicals 30%

Roman Catholics 25%

Protestant (Liberal) 20%

Protestant (African-Americans) 8%

Jewish 2%

Other 15%

Source: City University of New York, 2001)

The same study concluded that by most standards, the United States was a more professedly religious country than any European nations except Ireland and Poland.

Conservative belief

The religious convictions of Americans tend toward the conservative end of the spectrum.

An ABC new poll, done in February 2004, found that approximately 60% Of Americans believed that the Genesis creation account, Noah's ark, and a global flood, and Moses' parting of the Red Sea are literally true".

Belief in the literal veracity of these biblical accounts was highest among Evangelical Christians, the fastest growing segment of American faith.

How does such robust religious faith impact and influence American Government and the nation's domestic and foreign policies?

## Religious vote

An ABC news poll taken on Election Day 2000 found that among the voters who attended religious services at least once a week, 58% voted for Bush.

Conversely, Gore won 61% among the 14% of Americans who reported that they never attended religious services.

It is difficult to imagine the United States electing a candidate with the beliefs and policies of George W. Bush, or for that matter, Ronald Reagan, without the strong role an increasingly conservative faith plays in tens of millions' American lives.

Some estimates conclude that perhaps 40% of President Bush's total raw vote was provided by self-identified "evangelical" Christians.

## Religion and society

How does this deep and abiding religious belief impact upon American society?

According to an ICM poll in January 2004, Americans believe in the Supernatural (81%), an afterlife (74%), "belief in a God/ higher power makes you a better human being" (82%), God or a higher power judged your actions(76%), and perhaps most tellingly, "would die for their God/ beliefs".

In fact, only about 20% of Americans attend religious services in any given week .More than 50% never attend, aside from occasional funerals or weddings. Many were affiliated, at one time in their lives, with one of the more than 1,350 major minor denominations and sects in the United States, but have since allowed their membership to lapse .Meanwhile, millions of Americans who have intermarried with spouses of other faiths and that religious identity and church or temple membership may be a point of contention. Others find it a point of utter indifference. Millions more went to college, encountered new vistas in their thinking, and now harbor serious doubts about the truth of their religion-doubts which they often keep to themselves.

Indeed, the secular outlook is shared by countless men and women of every generation, from the famous to the ordinary, from all walks of life and from all over the world. Today, millions in England, France, Germany, and Italy, Eastern Europe, and Scandinavia, even Australia and Asia, are completely secular. Open-minded, democratic and tolerant, they seek to build the good life in this life and do not practice religion. In many countries of the world, religious believers are actually in the minority, and in those countries-sadly, unlike our own United States-the nonreligious do not face threats of condemnation by vociferous fundamentalists who are eager to condemn them to Hell.

According to a new study conducted by researchers at the University  of Minnesota Department of Sociology, atheists are identified as the United States' most distrusted minority. The study found that Americans rate atheists below Muslims, recent immigrants, gays and lesbians, and other minority groups in "sharing their vision of American society." Atheists are also the people least welcome to marry their children.

A relentless religious crusade is promoting a union of church and state, while attacking reproductive rights, gay rights, stem cell research, and death with dignity.

One thing we know with certainty.... These far-right organizations have

Had greater influence over the White House and the Congress in the past five years than at any other time in our nation's history! And they have used that influence to divide America and force their minority views and regressive policies on all of us.

1OO MILLION Americans listen to Christian radio, 43% more than five years ago.

During his first term in office, President George W. Bush ushered in "faith-based" initiatives-a fancy term for mandatory taxpayer-supported religion.

He also sought to stack the federal courts with judicial extremists who hate Church-state separation. One Bush judge even argued that America was meant to be a "Christian nation."

Zealots who follow aggressive TV preachers like Pat Robertson and Jerry Falwell are Bush's base. What do they want? Nothing less than a country that enforces fundamentalist religion by law.

Robertson and Falwell both shamefully blamed America's courts and the highest levels of our government for the horrific September 11 attacks on our nation. They said it happened because we "insulted God." Falwell went on to blame feminists, pro-choice Americans, and other groups he despises.

Hundreds of millions of people around the world no longer feel that the United States is a country that can be trusted. They feel the people who run the affairs of state are out of control and dangerous.

## FAMILY PLANNING

No fewer than 500,000 women die every year from pregnancy complications of giving birth. 99% of them occur in developing countries. In North America, one out of every 3700 women dies from pregnancy. In Africa it's one in 16. And in most of those countries, most women bear far more children than they want or are able to support. And maternal death leaves a tragic wake of motherless young children and plunges already fragile families further into poverty.

The need for family planning has never been greater. There are a staggering 120 million women who want family planning but have little or no access to it. Thruout the world, only one in 6 women of childbearing age has access to a broad range of contraceptive services.

Every day, 250,000 more people and every year 74 million are added to this environmentally overburdened planet. In the last 100 years, the world's population has quadrupled.

Surveys have shown 38% of all pregnancies are unwanted or mistimed. Every year, an estimated 80,000 women, one-fifth of all maternal deaths, are from complications of unsafe abortion. For every woman who dies from complications of pregnancy and childbirth, roughly 20 more suffer serious injury or disability.

The United Nations Population Fund has come to the rescue of 140 underdeveloped nations' family planning plight and the birth rates have fallen by half in these nations. Yet, despite overwhelming success, Bush has cancelled the promised $34 million yearly US contribution every year since 2002.

The agency estimates that lost US monies could have prevented 6 million unwanted pregnancies, 2.4 million abortions, and more than 14,000 maternal and 230,000 child deaths.

Consider, as well, the effects of the Global Gag Rule, imposed by the President 2 days after he took office for his first term. Under this rule, family planning groups on foreign soil can't receive US funds if they offer abortion services, including counseling and referrals. Nor lobby to make or keep abortion legal in their own countries..

Sadly, over 150 million married women in developing nations would like to delay the birth of their next child but lack the means to do so. And over 350 million couples worldwide don't have access to family planning services.

Emergency contraception in the form of a "morning after pill' named Plan B, which is an extra-strong birth control pill, prevents implantation of a fertilized egg if taken within 72 hours of unprotected sex. It has been found to be perfectly safe for use to women of childbearing age, and meets the requirements for being sold "over the counter," without a doctor's prescription. Yet, the Food and Drug Administration gutlessly yielded to anti-abortion groups and postponed allowing it to be sold over the counter.

This cowardly act by the FDA caused much outrage, especially by a few female US Senators, saying it was politically motivated. And Assistant Commissioner Dr. Susan Wood, Director of the FDA's Office of Women's Health, and Dr. Frank Davidoff, consultant to the FDA's Nonprescription Drugs Advisory Committee, resigned over it.

On resigning, Dr. Wood said, " As a scientist, as a career FDA employee, and as the director of the Office of

Women's Health, whose mission it is to be the champion for women's health at the FDA, I could not sanction this action by remaining at the agency. My role is to be the civil servant who has seen something go wrong and has to stand up and object.

Since 1999, the year the FDA made Plan B available by prescription, many states have made Plan B available over the counter. Also, Senators Clinton and Murray have vowed to block President Bush's nomination of a new commissioner to the FDA until the agency reverses its position on Plan B. So, the story isn't all bad.

## Abstinence

It's referred to as "Abstinence only Education", and since 1996, has resulted in myriads of federally funded and privately funded high school abstinence clubs across the land. Whose purpose is to sell virginity until marriage to boys and girls alike. Millions of dollars a year support it, coming from not only Bush's budget, but also well-to-do folks, mainly members of the religious right.

Virginity pledges were introduced in the early 1990s as part of the Christian Sex Education Project. Their adult champions hail the promises, which rest solely on the individual's word, as being a major step toward reducing teen pregnancy and raising moral values. But many others have pooh-poohed its value.

By some estimates, at least 2.5 million adolescents around the world have publicly vowed to postpone sex until marriage. They include virgins as well as those who have had a sexual experience but swear to refrain from further activity.

Many wear rings or other jewelry to symbolize their pledge.

It has been a subject of much controversy, pro and con,

whether it works or not, since its beginning. A Harvard University study interviewing 14,000 survey subjects, age 12 to 18, in 1995 and again in 1996 and 2001, and had lived throughout the US, found that 52% had had sex within a year. Additionally 73% of those who told the 1st survey that they had taken a pledge but later had sex, denied making such a promise when they were surveyed a 2nd time.

It was concluded that there was a lot of error in these studies and that medical testing is more reliable than the adolescents' own reporting. Also, the virginity pledges have little staying power.

### Roe v. Wade

Fortune finally smiled of the lives of US women in 1973 when the Supreme

Court legalized abortion, saving thousands from death and injury by back alley abortionists, or fleeing to countries such as Japan, where abortion was legal. But,

Now George Bush has appointed 2 probable pro-life members to the court, and states like South Dakota have banned abortion, pro-choice advocates can't relax.

And as if that isn't bad enough, pro-lifers are doing their utmost to place road blocks in many states, which would prevent safe, legal abortions. Such as the over than 650 bills introduced by legislators in all 50 states, that would limit, inhibit, or even ban access to abortion, contraception, and other fundamental reproductive rights. And criminalizing procedures as early as the 12th week of pregnancy. 24 states have enacted 36 such laws.

In 2005 the deceptive federal "Partial Birth Abortion Ban Act" was declared unconstitutional because it failed to provide any health exceptions and constituted a significant health hazard. And states have passed their own partial abortion ban acts. One vetoed bill stated that aborting at

8 weeks of pregnancy could have allowed a first-degree murder charge!!

Other laws require parental or judicial consent under age 17. Some young women, if forced to talk to their parents about abortion, would face physical or emotional abuse. Or get an illegal back alley abortion. Another law would require the health care provider to notify the parent or guardian 48 hours prior to the procedure for females under 18, or for the woman to obtain a court waiver of the requirement.

Many states have found an insidious way to promote anti-choice politics—using taxpayer money to make and distribute license plates with "CHOOSE LIFE" printed on them. And some states have refused to create 'Pro-Choice" plates.

Many states have passed laws allowing pharmacists to refuse to fill birth control prescriptions based on personal moral or religious objections. And some pharmacists even refuse to refer women to another pharmacy-or to transfer the prescription. Despite the fact that 95% of women in the US take birth control at some point in their lives.

## THE WIDENING GAP BETWEEN

## RICH AND POOR

Poverty is defined as annual income relative to family size. For instance, in the 48 contiguous states and D.C., less than $19,350 is the minimum annual income necessary for a family of 4 to be defined as living in poverty. In Alaska and Hawaii, the dollar amount is higher. 37 million or 12.7% of the US population is now living in poverty, and shamefully, the US poverty rate ranks number one among developed nations. On the other hand, the US ranks #1 in the number of billionaires.

The US minimum wage is $5.15 an hour, or about $10,500 a year, poverty pay, and in spite of the continuing rise in the cost of living, it hasn't been increased since 1997!! And while Congress has refused to raise the minimum wage, it has Increased its own pay every year for the past 8 years, to a present total of $168,500.

There are 7.3 million Americans working for the minimum wage. Another 8.2 million are paid only $1 more than the minimum. 72% of minimum wage workers are adults. One third of them are the family's only income provider. 60% of these workers are women and 760,000 are single moms.

### Taxes

A study of the 2001-enacted Bush tax cut shows that over the ten year period the richest Americans---the best-off !%- are slated to receive tax cuts totaling almost half a trillion dollars. The $477 billion in tax breaks the Bush administration has targeted to this elite group will average $342,000 each over the decade.

By 2010, when the Bush tax cuts are fully in place, 52% of the total tax cuts will go to the richest 1%, whose average 2010 income will be $1.5 million.

The tax-cut windfall in that year will average $65,000 each. Putting it another way, of the estimated $234 billion scheduled in tax cuts for the year 2010, $121 billion will go to just 1.4 million taxpayers.

If you make $1 million-plus a year, the tax bill enacted in 2006 will save you an additional $43,000; if you make $ 40 to 50,000 a year, you'll get$47—enough for a tank of gas. Bush's tax plan promises you next to nothing.

Richard Greenstein of the Center on Budget and Policy Priorities said," This indefensible agreement provides a windfall for the most well-off, little or nothing for most other Americans, relies on budget gimmicks to help mask its long term costs, and will further increase our already large and unsustainable deficits."

The Bush ax plan is not a "tax cut" but a "tax shift". It shifts $70 billion of the tax burden away from the wealthy (and corporations) and onto workers and low-income people.

## The US Drug Problem

Almost every government except the US bargains over drug prices, and the Congressional Budget Office says that foreign drug prices are 30 to 55% below US levels. Even in the US, Veterans Affairs is able to negotiate discounts of 50% or more, far more than the Medicare actuary expects the elderly to receive under the current plan. And the law specifically prohibits Medicare from using its purchasing power to negotiate lower drug prices. But, many seniors get around it by buying drugs from Canada, which are cheaper.

Needless to say, apologists for the law insist that prohibition on price negotiations say it had nothing to do with catering to special interests, that it was a matter of principle, of preserving incentives to innovate. But the experts show convincingly that drug companies spend far more on marketing than they do on research.

## Medicaid Loses Out

Created in 1985 as part of Lyndon Johnson's Great Society, Medicaid Is structured so that the feds pay a share of each state's cost of caring for disabled Americans. But, as tax cuts lessened the states' income and millions of Americans found themselves unable to afford health insurance, Medicaid became more and more used to pay for health care. But, state budgets, suffering from tax cuts and recession, were unable to cover their share of Medicaid costs. So, many states made it more difficult to qualify for Medicaid and cut benefits. And, unfortunately, the disabled were the losers.

### Social Security Going Broke?

Since most Americans are against privatization of Social Security, Bush's plan to privatize it is dead. But, many predict Social Security is doomed as the baby boomers reach 65. What should be done to keep Social Security alive?

Even after all the government bonds in the Trust Fund are retired in 2042 or 2052,there will be enough money coming into the system to pay 70 to 80% of benefits. But what about the unfunded balance?

No problem. Increase the amount of salary subject to S.S. tax from the current $90,000 to $200,000 or more. And, increase the amount the wage earner and the employer contribute from 6.2 to 6.5%. Also, since Americans are living and able to work longer, maybe the age S.S. starts should be later.

### The Overall Economy

The budget surplus Bush inherited in 2001 when he came into office was $5.6 trillion. And the Senate voted 52-48 to go along with Bush's demand that the legal ceiling on the national debt be raised to $9 billion for 2006. This amounts to roughly $30,000 owed by every man, woman, and child.

### Tax Insanity

In an era of massive budget deficits, it makes little sense for the US to continue the present tax cuts for the rich, which reduced the tax rate of 38.6% on dividends and capital gains held almost exclusively by the wealthy, to 15%. This law, originally due to expire in 2008, is being extended and will now expire in 2010,returning the rate to its former figure of 38.5%

Since the top 1% of income earners take home more than the bottom 100 Million, not only should the top marginal tax rates be restored to the Nixon-era level of 70%, but wealth taxes that are common in Europe, should be instituted in the US. And corporate tax policies of the Eisenhower era, when corporations accounted for roughly 25% of federal revenues, instead of today's 10%, should be brought back.

# EDUCATION

## Public Schools

K-12 schools are suffering from many unfortunate recent developments.

Topping the list of complaints by many leading educators, researchers, teachers, and administrators is George Bush's "No Child Let Behind" (NCLB) It is claimed that it threatens to close more than 6,000 public schools, being a stealth campaign to privatize US public education, pushing dedicated teachers and disadvantaged children out of our neighborhood schools and forcing financially strapped schools to squander meager resources on high stakes standardized tests.

It shifts control of every aspect of public education to a faceless Washington bureaucracy, while marginalizing successful methods, materials, teacher education, staff development programs, and curriculum. It's responsible for the government blacklisting successful professors, institutions, methods, and materials that deviate from the NCLB party line. George Bush's top education advisors call the National Education Association members "terrorists"" and would like to 'blow up" teachers' colleges.

Only 3 states have not in some way challenged NCLB's extension of federal supervision over grades K thru 12, but no state has done so with as much brio as Utah, which is insurrectionary, even tho last year 87% of its schools fulfilled NCLB's requirement of showing "adequate yearly progress." Utah's objection is based on "sovereignty". It is the only state that largely continues to live by the teachings of a church. They believe they have high community standards and that their schools and universities adhere to them. They might be wrong, but they think that under federalism, it is their right to be wrong.

The Bush Administration calls the 1,100-page NCLB law "the most Important federal education reform in history". It is a federal attempt at large-scale behavior modification, using sunlight to cause embarrassment to prompt reform.

Their reasons for a continental nation often collide with regional differences. NCLB In effect says, "If you keep doing what you have been doing, you won't get better."

They claim the poor are still not learning as they should. That gaps between the cognitive attainments of many disadvantaged are as wide as ever, and a definition of insanity is "Doing the same thing over and over and expecting the results to be different."

Meanwhile, the Bush Administration was taken to task for reportedly reneging $40 billion on the NCLB Act.

And leaving 5 million children behind in spite of the clear commitment to leave no child behind. Also, not funding the Individuals with Disabilities in Education Act as promised.

Public education experts believe that before the mean-spirited test-driven attack on public education began to kick in, the US had much to be proud of in public ed, such as free access to education from all economic levels and racial backgrounds; an increasingly high percentage finishing secondary schools; a higher rate of youth reaching and completing some level of higher ed than any other nation; and an increasingly professional staff, research and theory making it possible for a wider range to succeed and be motivated to stay in school.

Now, they despair over the lack of support for education that has led to decaying facilities, a shortage of professional teachers, unequal support depending whether the school is located in poor or upper income districts, uncertified teachers, outdated and insufficient supplies, teachers blamed for failures in the system, and politicians 'disrespect for teachers.

The present condition of US public schools amounts to a crisis that the world's richest nation should be ashamed of and should not allow to continue. All of US society should be mobilized to correct the situation as soon as possible. Our youth are our most precious asset and deserve the best, not the mediocrity that has befallen them.

## Higher Ed

The world's richest nation can't afford to pay the tuition, even for the poorest students? But, some EU nations can? All the US can afford to pay are low Interest loans for tuition? What a travesty!

The figures are depressing. Only 3% of students in the top 146 colleges come from families in the bottom income quartile. Only 10% come from the bottom half. The cost of going to college is rising and so is student debt. Over the past 4 years, the cost of attending a public 4-year college has increased 32% , while the median family income has risen less than 6%. As a result of tuition jumps, 62% of undergraduates are taking out loans, with the average debt totaling $19,800.

In 2002, the Republican-controlled Congress seemed indifferent to the problem, directing $12 billion in savings from changes to federal student aid programs to deficit reduction instead of additional student assistance. In that year, Congress boosted the student loan rate to a fixed 6.5% and the rate on new loans to 8.5%.

In the 1950s, fewer than 1 in 10 US workers were college educated. Between 1965-1985, these numbers increased by over 300%.. Today, more than 30% of the US workforce possess a Bachelor of Arts or better. In the past 20 years, however, growth has been limited to a mere 20%, and since 2000, it has flattened altogether.

Academic professionals are feeling the disadvantage that the humanities have in the marketplace. Unlike fields such as medicine, the sciences, and engineering, there is little federal or state support provided to the humanities. Yet, they feel a university cannot be great by unless teaching and scholarship in the humanities are great. They are also disturbed by university bureaucracy they call medieval because so much time, like 100 hours, is having to prepare an interminable application. Then going thru committee after committee in the promotion process.

Another problem causing hardship for both students and faculty is the skyrocketing cost of textbooks; up to $500 for a single semester's textbook!

We should bring back the G.I. Bill. After WWII, nearly 8 million veterans received benefits for college, technical, or agricultural educations. Let's do it again, extending it only to lower income persons. Today, it costs a state $24,000 to put a student through a one-year course, which returns about $2 million to the state's economy during the student's work life.

## THE ENVIRONMENT

Probably the most definitive critique of what the US government is doing and not doing, re the environment, comes from the pen of Robert F. Kennedy, Jr. in his current book, Crimes Against Nature . As the country's most prominent environmental attorney, Kennedy condemns the Bush Administration for eviscerating the laws that have protected our nation's air, water, public lands, and wildlife for the past 30 years, enriching the president's political contributors, while lowering the quality of life for the rest of us.

Kennedy lifts the veil on how the administration has orchestrated these rollbacks, almost entirely outside of public scrutiny—and in tandem with the very industries our laws are meant to regulate, the country's most notorious polluters.

He reports on how the White House doles out lavish subsidies and tax breaks to the energy barons while excusing industry from providing adequate security at the more than 15, 000 chemical and nuclear facilities that are prime targets for terrorist attacks.

In his 2nd chapter, Kennedy says that when the postwar industrial boom arrived, Americans found themselves paying a high price for the resulting pollution.

The wake-up call came in the late 1960s, when Lake Erie was declared dead.

Cleveland's Cuyahoga River caught fire, and radioactive strontium 90 was found in mothers' breast milk across America. 40% of US waters became undrinkable, unfishable, and unswimmable. And thousands of Americans died each year when smog broke out.

Pesticides nearly extinguished the mid-Atlantic populations of ospreys, herons, and bald eagles, as well as some of the songbirds. And peregrine falcons were poisoned out of existence by DDT. The Clean Air Act and the Endangered Species Act followed, making corporate polluters accountable, and was reinforced by Earth Day 1970, when 20 million Americans poured into the streets for the largest demonstration in US history.

But, over the next 30 years, the polluters mounted an increasingly sophisticated and aggressive counterattack to undermine the laws. The environmental reversals of the Bush administration are the triumphant outcome of their 3-decade campaign. In 1976, the Colorado brewer Joseph Coors founded the Mountain States Legal Foundation to challenge environmental laws, and was funded by multinational polluters such as Phillips Petroleum, Exxon, Texaco, Amoco, Shell, Ford Motor Company, and Chevron. Coors also founded the right-wing Heritage Foundation to provide philosophical underpinning for the anti-environmental Movement.

The most prominent of the many pro-environmental organizations in the US is the Natural Resources Defense Council, with 500, 000 members and Kennedy as senior attorney. This organization and many others are doing very good work bringing us a better environment.

In addition to global warming, they are fighting toxic pollution, which is causing a near epidemic of childhood asthma, industrial fishing practices which destroy the ocean floor, and kill 300,000 dolphins and whales each year. And, protecting animal habitats and wildlife, such as the Florida panther, grey wolf, grizzly bear, and other living things, which are in danger of being lost forever. And protecting forests, lakes, coastlines, and National Parks from illegal logging and drilling for oil. And opposing urban sprawl from draining and filling over wetlands, paving over prairies, and mining pollution and preventing mercury, DDT, and cancer-causing trichloroethylene and other harmful chemicals from entering the water supply.

The outlook for improving the environment in the near future does not look good. Especially, as long as the Bush Administration is in power. The only solution is for Americans en masse to raise their voices to overcome the deep pockets and political clout of the oil industry, logging and mining companies, developers, and other anti-environmental special interests. And hope that the next US president will support a vigorous Environmental Protection Agency, and not run over it in the way the Bush Administration has done.

## IMMIGRATION : Anti-Immigration Antics

Sadly, US anti-immigration action has recently mushroomed, including a Congressional bill making it a felony in the US without proper documentation, calls for constructing a 2,000-mile wall between the US and Mexico. A wall intended to keep Mexicans out of the territory, which was violently taken from Mexico in the War of 1846-1848. And self-styled " Minutemen" and similar groups with guns, patrolling the border.

Unfortunately, this "border war" debate tends to obscure factors such as the Constitution, which guarantees "due process" and " equal protection" to all persons, whether US citizens or not.

Also, there are several commonly-myths regarding immigrants that need debunking. Myth #1: Immigrants take jobs away from Americans. Myth #2: Most Immigrants are a drain on the economy or treasury. Myth #3: America is being overrun by immigrants. Myth #4: Immigrants aren't really interested in becoming part of American society. Myth #5: immigrants contribute little to American society.

These myths are contradicted by solid facts and extensive studies conducted by professionals and irrefutable logic.

In the past, Americans have treated several immigrant groups in a most uncivilized fashion. Such as the anti-Irish sentiment in the 1840s and 50s after the failure of Ireland's potato crop, which killed a million and drove millions abroad. And the Chinese Exclusion Act of 1882, after these hard-working people had heroically built our first transcontinental railroad. And the deportation of 249 non-citizens of Russian descent, supervised by young J. Edgar Hoover, after the 1917 Bolshevik Revolution when a bomb exploded in front of the house of the US attorney general.

And the 1924 National Origins Quota Act limiting immigrants from Eastern and Southern Europe.

The pro-Immigration demonstrations in the US in cities across the country remind us of the compassionate Statute of Liberty words: " Give me your tired, your poor, your huddled masses yearning to breathe free, the wretched refuse of your teeming shore. Send these, the homeless, tempest tossed, to me. I lift my lamp beside the golden door."

The perfect opportunity for the richest, most powerful nation has arrived to show the many hostile, alienated world populations that the US is not really uncivilized and uncaring about the suffering and deprivation of the poverty stricken members of other countries. In other words, the US should react compassionately and understandingly toward the millions of undocumented immigrants within its borders.

That means no punitive anti-immigration Congressional legislation. No militarization of the Mexican border. No criminalization of illegals. No employer sanctions. Yes to amnesty for undocumented workers. Yes to immigrant family reunification. Yes to a humane path to citizenship. Yes to labor rights and living wages for all workers.

# CONCLUSION

The fact that the Bush Administration is out of step with the rest of the world positions the US indifferent to the realities of population trends that will ultimately affect every one of us. With a population of 6.5 billion, the world is already straining its resources to the limit. Yet, we will continue to grow by nearly 80 billion people a year. By 2050, world population is expected to reach 9.2 billion. Of that 8 billion will inhabit developing countries. There won't be enough food, clean water, and other life necessities to care for them. The result will be a permanent nightmare of widespread poverty, armed conflict, disease, pestilence, and massive migration.

To mitigate these threats, we should act now, establishing programs that work!!

First of all, we, the world's richest country, must contribute our share, reversing Bush's irresponsible actions re family planning. Without contraception, the average woman would bear between 12 and 15 children in her lifetime. 200 million worldwide are estimated to become pregnant each year, but 80 million of these are unplanned. Unintended pregnancies result in 19 million unsafe abortions annually, worldwide. Pregnancy-related causes kill 530,000 women annually. This must change!

Next, we must correct the awful situation of 815 people, 200 million of them are children suffering from hunger and malnutrition. 115 million children are not attending primary school, 1.1 billion are unable to depend on safe drinking water, and more than 1 billion people are living on less than $1 a day.

Studies show that whenever a woman has achieved

an 8<sup>th</sup> grade education, she has about half the number of pregnancies as women with no education. While every child in the world is entitled to least a basic education, young girls historically, have been denied this opportunity.

Finally, we should correct our own deficiencies, including adequate family services to correct the fact that half of all pregnancies are unintended, shooting for the Dutch abortion rate of 6.5 per thousand per yea, instead of ours, which is 22.9 per thousand per year, and the Dutch teen pregnancy rate. Ours is 9 times higher than theirs. And the teen gonorrhea rate which is an astounding 74 times higher than theirs. And providing real, thorough sex ed beginning before teenage. And requiring every emergency room to prescribe emergency contraception for rape victims. And requiring health insurance companies to include birth control.

How in the world, even after the Bush Administration is gone, the religious right still as powerful and malignant as ever, can all this be achieved? Yes, it looks like too high a mountain to climb. But it must be attempted. And with determination and resolve it is doable!

The western world has seen the rise and fall of several great empires. The Greek Athenian empire lasted about 4 centuries, and was replaced by the thousand-year Roman empire.

The next great empire to dominate not only the western world but worldwide was the British wempire lasting from the early 1600s to WWII. After that came the US empire, the world's first superpower.

Thing went well for the US for some time after that, only marred by anticommunist hysteria including the McCarthy era when many prominent citizens were foolishly punished by reputation or job loss. And the Vietnam War, a big mistake, lost because the US didn't have the patience to fight a guerilla war of dubious cause. And the Iraq war was in the same category.

At the same time, the US gradually lost world respect because it stopped cooperating with the UN and many of its functions including the Kyoto Protocol on global warming, the International Court at the Hague, the Geneva Convention against torture, the land mine treaty, abolishing the death penalty, denying foreigners, who are being prosecuted in the US, access to their own nations' help, etc.

At the same time, the US has lost much credibility and respect, internationally, because of domestic issues differing from those of other industrialized nations. Such as laws re gay Rights, same sex marriage, legalized marijuana, lax gun control, Legalized prostitution, euthanasia, stem cell research, legalized Abortion, universal health care, etc., either nationally or varying state by state.

How can we explain such differences from other advanced nations' policies and philosophies?

The most important reason is that we are a nation of immigrants, many of whose ancestors came to this country because they didn't have the skills or intellect to make a good living at home. And consequently went inland to our central states where they did very well farming. But were susceptible to the wily wiles of masterful orators like Billy Graham, Pat Robertson, Oral Roberts, Jerry Falwell, and their fundamentalist Christian mythology. And voted for like-minded George W. Bush.

Unless we change our anti-international attitude, it is likely that the rest of the world, despising us for our failings, and because the US empire is based on wealth and military strength, will unite non-militarily against us and erode and diminish our power, ending the US empire.

We must not let this happen. We must change our attitude and actions as soon as possible. We have much to offer the rest of the world, especially the undeveloped nations. We could easily regain the respect, honor, and leadership we used to have if we adopt the rational, cooperative, civilized, up-to-date international demeanor we once showed the rest of the world.

There are, of course, other issues not covered in this book, where the US has gone wrong. Such as the Patriot Act and Bush breaking the law requiring a court order before wiretapping. And corruption involving Congressmen and lobbyists. And the Robber Oil Barons. But, most of the shameful issues are covered. Hopefully, most of these failings will be rectified as US citizens in this new age of communication gain the insight that other more enlightened nations already possess, making this expose and its revelations herein irrelevant. And the sooner the better.

And it's to be hoped that this book hastens progress towards this end, bringing the US one step closer to utopia!

www.ingramcontent.com/pod-product-compliance
Lightning Source LLC
Chambersburg PA
CBHW031237280526
45784CB00004B/1613